Days In The Life

John Lennon Remembered

Days in the Life

John Lennon Remembered

Philip Norman

CENTURY

LONDON SYDNEY AUCKLAND JOHANNESBURG

Designed by Paul Bowden Design
Picture research by Susan Ready

Text copyright © Philip Norman 1990
Photographs copyright © copyright owners, see page 120

First published in 1990 by Random Century Ltd,
Random Century House, 20 Vauxhall Bridge Road, London SW1V 2SA

Random Century Australia Pty Ltd,
20 Alfred Street, Milsons Point, Sydney, NSW 2061 Australia

Random Century New Zealand Ltd
9-11 Rothwell Avenue, Albany
Private Bag, North Shore Mail Centre, Glenfield, Auckland 10 New Zealand

Century Hutchinson South Africa Pty Ltd,
PO Box 337, Bergvlei 2012 South Africa

British Library Cataloguing in Publication Data
Norman, Philip 1943 -
Days in the life : John Lennon Remembered
1. Pop Music. Lennon, John, 1940 -1980
1. Title
782.42164092

ISBN 0 - 7126 - 3922 - 5

Printed and bound in Great Britain by Butler and Tanner Ltd.,
Frome and London

'You must have known him well,' people often say to me.

'Not well,' I'm forced to admit. 'Of course, I met him a couple of times – but then, so did umpteen hundred other people. I was never what you'd call a friend. I mean, I never tried to know him, or anyone like that. And yet I ended up knowing him so incredibly well...knowing more about him, perhaps, than even he did...'

People at this point look understandably puzzled. The best course is, shut up now. Or tell the whole complicated and slightly absurd story.

In 1962 I was aged nineteen; just one of the crowd, a long way at the back. I had recently left school without benefit of further education, and become an apprentice reporter on the *Hunts Post*, 'County Newspaper for Huntingdonshire'. It was a job of mind-numbing tedium. I had almost no friends, and no girl friend. My dress was shabby, my social standing low. Sometimes, after my day's work on the County Newspaper for Huntingdonshire, I would take out my wallet and wish I could just crawl into one of its pockets and hide.

My temporary lodging was a rambling old farmhouse, marooned among fields of East Anglia's chief agricultural products, the cabbage and the Brussels sprout. Some aberration in its past had given the house an opulent bathroom tiled in royal blue like some Irving Thalberg mansion in Hollywood. It was in this blue Thalberg bathroom in the East Anglian wilds that I first heard The Beatles' Love Me Do.

Like many other people, I wasn't sure at first if it was a serious Pop record. You must appreciate that British Pop, in 1962, had a form as rigidly constrained as the sonnet or haiku. It was sung by lisping boys next door, backed by 'groups' with solid Fender Stratocaster guitars, modelled after Cliff Richard's Shadows. Mocked and vilified since the time of Elvis Presley, it survived only by maintaining a low and respectful profile. The tight little dance-routine performed by The Shadows themselves summed up the prevailing mood of formulaic inhibition: one step left, one right, one forward, one back, one tentative little kick of goblin-toed boot.

What was one to make of a record that so obviously broke every rule for commercial success? Instead of massed guitars, a single, wheezy harmonica. Instead of lead vocals by someone named Cliff, Billy or Shane, two voices mixed: a flat, nasal one singing the bottom line, and a higher one, chiming 'Whoa-oh.. love me do..' An odd, shuffling stop-start beat. And, of course, the sheer self-defeating absurdity of their name. 'That one from The Beat-les...' the BBC announcer intoned amusedly, as if sharing my own conviction they'd never be heard from again.

My mother was then a beautician, working at a department store in Norwich, some eighty miles away. Her man friend – the farmer with whom I was staying – would sometimes drive me up to see her at weekends in his blue Ford Zodiac. It was on one of these journeys that I first heard The Beatles' Please Please Me.

It was a sunny winter Sunday morning, just before noon. We had become trapped in a long queue of traffic going to the motor races at Snetterton. The car-radio was tuned to one of the BBC's few Pop music programmes, Brian Matthew's Easy Beat. My mother's farmer friend enjoyed Pop music, though he disliked Pop singers. He would make up his own words to songs, for example singing 'Rigor Rigor Rigor-la-Mortis' to The Shadows instrumental F.B.I.

Just before Please Please Me began, my mother's farmer friend had lost patience with the queue and attempted to jump it by driving straight down the empty oncoming lane. He would have succeeded but for a bottle green E-Type Jaguar, which pulled out crosswise to block his path, the checkered sleeve of its driver waving him furiously back. With traffic coming the other way again, he had no choice but to mount the opposite verge, robbed of his place in the queue, and unable to get across to rejoin it.

I remember the rich confusion of that moment; the curses of my mother's farmer friend; the prick of stubble on my half-shaved face in the hot sun; the roar of racing cars beyond the hedge. And from the radio, the same eccentrically mixed-up voices as before, but newly focused and energised, singing words that seemed a derisive comment on our thoroughly deserved predicament: 'Come on! Come on! Come on! Come on! Come on! Come on! Come on!...'

There are some things which at any age one knows beyond any doubt. As the voices climbed to that eighth 'Come on', then toppled over into falsetto - 'Please please me, whoa yeah!' - I knew beyond a doubt they had a hit, and felt a tug of happiness, despite everything. We teenagers of 1963 were an embattled species. Any success of youth counted as success in common.

★

I saw them first on a television Pop show called Thank Your Lucky Stars, also presented by Brian Matthew. A respected senior broadcaster now, Matthew was then our nearest approach to Dick Clark or Alan Freed, presiding over almost all British broadcasting's tiny Pop output with the air of a faintly irritable schoolmaster. This he would attempt to moderate by wearing dark polo-necked woollens inside pale V-necked ones, and referring to himself, not with total conviction, as 'Yer old mate Brian Matthew'.

Though Please Please Me was number two in the charts, one still felt unsure whether to take them quite seriously. For every necessary visual component of a Pop group seemed to have been perversely left out. Hair, not swept up and back but combed forward in a fringe like the fall guy in the Three Stooges. Jacket-fronts, not plunging to fasten with cloth-covered link buttons, but circling the neck in the feminine mode of Chanel. Guitars, not flat and electric but bulky and acoustic, the bass played left-handed, a strange, attenuated violin shape. Faces, not gaunt and moody but round and happy and split by unprecedented broad grins. One instantly noticed the grin of the one on the right; its faint but unmistakable air of mockery.

Their names were another break with tradition, which specified that male Pop stars must have pseudonyms suggestive of tempestuous passion or moody low-burning fire. Theirs were not only real but unashamedly commonplace: John, Paul and George - in that order from the very beginning. And a nickname, Ringo, suggesting playground cowboy games. Ordinary, yet not so, as one had begun to realise by their third single, From Me To You. 'Like their previous release,' I read in the *New Musical Express*, 'both A and B-sides were written by guitarist John Lennon and bass-player Paul McCartney...' In those days, I detested my own name, and was always trying on other peoples'. 'McCartney', I could not take quite seriously, since it was also the surname of Huntingdon's mayoress. But I fancied the sleekness of 'Lennon', especially against curt, straightforward 'John'.

To like The Beatles at the very beginning was to be embattled as never before. For six months, the adult world poured scorn on their music, hair and dress, fulminated against their supposed malign influence on 'young people', held them up as the epitome of Britain's post-imperial decline. My colleagues at the County Newspaper for Huntingdonshire - Traditional Jazz fans to a man - sang a daily hymn of hate. The women were equally anti, all except one sympathique married one in Classified Ads, who admitted that 'if you look below the hair, their faces are really quite sensitive'. To my mother's farmer friend, they were a scourge as bad as pigeons on Brussels sprouts. I remember him showing me the *Daily Express* story about their ejection from a Young Conservatives dance in Carlisle, for the sin of wearing black leather jackets. 'Nasty little things,' he murmured as he went off to his tractor again. 'Nast-y little things.'

What changed everything was that wet summer of 1963, when the Profumo scandal broke and Britain's public life was exposed as a rank cheese, crawling with maggots. Exhausted by incessant upper-class sex and seediness, Fleet Street took up The Beatles as the only available source of innocent light relief. By the year's end, the disreputable leather jacket-wearers were performing before The Queen Mother at the London Palladium. John Lennon had gained his first solo headline by requesting those in the cheaper sets to clap and those in the expensive ones - including the Royal Box - to 'rattle yer jewellery'.

Even at that early stage, one seemed to sense him chafing against his role. His Beatle fringe was always a little damp and ragged, the top button of his shirt frequently left undone. While George and Paul shared a microphone, he always sang into one on his own, slightly hunched and resigned over his black Rickenbacker 'Short arm'. Chorusing the 'yeah yeah' doggerel, his narrow-eyed face could at times resemble a Chinese waiter whose outward impassivity masks deep desire to bury an axe in some obstreperous customer's head.

After the flattened rasp of his singing, his speaking voice was surprisingly deep and lugubrious. He was funny at every moment, yet never nasty, even with the most insensate BBC blimp. 'John - why do you call yourselves The Beatles?' 'Er, well. It's just a name, you know. Like "shoe".' When his book, *A Spaniard In The Works*, was published, an over earnest interviewer asked if he made 'conscious use of onomatopoeia'. 'Automatic pier?' the glum voice echoed. 'I just haven't a clue what you're talking about.'

He was, one knew, the main reason Pop music started to be humorous; why it started to be vaguely intellectual; why it suddenly took large strides up the social register. Beatles albums ceased to be for working and lower middle class youth only, and began to be heard at County debutantes' New Year dances in blow-heated Tudor barns. I, too, had briefly moved up a class, walking out with a girl who wore navy blue with pink and her hair in a matching pink Alice band. For paralytically-inhibited 20 year-olds like me, Lennon's was the acceptable voice of male romance; that way he would address his inamorata with rough tenderness as 'Girl'. When I hear him sing Anna, on the *Please Please Me*

album, I am back in the world of Young Farmers and Hunt Balls, smooching with my Alice-banded love in the library of a house called Merton Grange.

Boys whose girl friends showed enthusiasm for Pop stars were traditionally obliged to go off into tempestuous sulks. One still did, of course, if one's date went gooey for Paul; but with John Lennon, it was different. He was not in the least pretty; girls, rather, said they found him 'interesting'. Somehow, they were always the darker, more obliquely attractive girls whom I hoped would find me 'interesting', too.

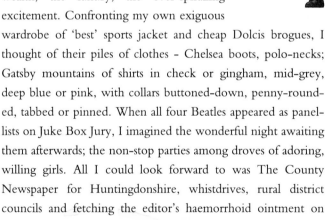

Myself, I did not care which one I swapped lives with: John, Paul, George, even the runtish Ringo. I would gaze longingly at the cover of *With The Beatles*, its four fringed faces in half shadow like soulful art students. How I envied that miraculous existence, cupped in simple polo-necks; the wealth, the luxury, the ever-spiralling excitement. Confronting my own exiguous wardrobe of 'best' sports jacket and cheap Dolcis brogues, I thought of their piles of clothes - Chelsea boots, polo-necks; Gatsby mountains of shirts in check or gingham, mid-grey, deep blue or pink, with collars buttoned-down, penny-rounded, tabbed or pinned. When all four Beatles appeared as panellists on Juke Box Jury, I imagined the wonderful night awaiting them afterwards; the non-stop parties among droves of adoring, willing girls. All I could look forward to was The County Newspaper for Huntingdonshire, whistdrives, rural district councils and fetching the editor's haemorrhoid ointment on Fridays. I was at the very back of the crowd.

By 1965, they had conquered the planet. Even my mother's farmer friend went around singing Help! with his own made-up lyrics. 'Nast-y lit-tle things,' he would sing, instead of 'Help in an-y way'.

Calling a song Help! seemed just another brilliant idea, from the one now recognised as having most of the ideas. It was obviously John Lennon, speaking in jokey thought-bubbles from a *Beano* comic-strip. Neither I nor any other of the bewitched millions recognised it as a genuine, anguished cri-de-coeur. How could we when the movie *Help!* so perfectly visualised the fun of being Beatles? Going through the front doors of four separate terrace houses, and arriving in a communal luxury pad, complete with high-fashion conversation-pit. Skylarking in the Swiss mountains. Skylarking in the Bermuda surf. Emerging from all adventures unscathed and unmarked like the Disney characters they had become. John seemed to personify it all, spooning soup into which, at the dictates of the

wacky Oriental plot, mysterious objects kept falling. 'What's that?' someone asked. 'A season ticket' John, expressionless, replied. I cannot adequately convey the effect of his bone-dry, deadpan style on my wet and woozy 22 year-old mind. It was as stinging, eye-opening and clarifying as a first taste of sex or champagne.

To look back to 1965 now is to see The Beatles' break-up already well under way. Even *Help!* with its one-for-all-and-all-for-one zaniness, has a moment of Lennon apostasy, the acrid 'Hey!' in You've Got To Hide Your Love Away. Then, all of a sudden, McCartney was recording Yesterday solo with a string quartet. And pirate Pop radio was playing the first song written, not from a puppy-lover's bedroom but a grown-up analyst's couch. It was John's Norwegian Wood, that edgy morning-after confession through Indian sitars like jangling nerve-ends. Even today it defies classification, poised between bravado and timidity, lust and self-disgust.

I myself had by now left The County Newspaper for Huntingdonshire, and exchanged the flat lands of East Anglia

for the industrial haze of Tyneside, 200 miles to the north. The Beatles' mid-season comes back to me in company with coal-mining towns, giant slag-heaps and the singsong Geordie accent that called them 'Bittles'. Help! reminds me of Darlington with its beige-and-blue buses and the model of George Stephenson's 'Locomotion No. 1' on a plinth at the railway station. Their album *Rubber Soul* reminds me of Newcastle, with streets plunging like cobbled waterfalls down to the River Tyne. I saw my first copy in W.H.Smith's window on my way to cover an inquest at the Swing Bridge. The four fringed faces subtly changed yet again, modishly distorted by a fisheye lens. Lucky Lennon, I thought, to be wearing that collarless and epauletted brown suede jacket.

To be a reporter in Newcastle was suddenly to be much nearer the front of the crowd. Late in 1966, on what no one suspected was to be their farewell British tour, The Beatles appeared at the City Hall. Head office in Darlington told me to cover the concert, adding 'See if you can get a word with them'.

Half a dozen of us, local hacks and national 'stringers' waited in a sooty Tyneside drizzle outside the City Hall's Stage Door. It was the first time I had ever seen streets packed from shopfronts to kerbside, as for some Coronation or State funeral. I do not remember screams or any noise, but a profound, almost eerie quiet.

Shortly after seven, a black Austin Princess limousine drew up. Paul got out first, then Ringo, then George, then John. To my disappointment, he was not at all smart. He wore a leather Lenin cap and a baggy white T-shirt marked 'Surf City', with no jacket. He carried a studentish sheaf of papers and books. While the others ran past, ignoring us, he wagged a finger and said 'A-ah, there you are!' as if he'd caught us playing Granny's Footsteps.

Regulated by stewards and bouncers like sets of traffic lights, we finally reached the corridor outside their dressing-room. Here we received polite discouragement from a man with crinkly blond hair, wearing immensely long and pointed black suede shoes. It was Tony Barrow, press officer for Brian Epstein's NEMS organisation, whose stylish releases used to circulate even as far as me on the County Newspaper for Huntingdonshire. One I particularly remember showed Epstein's head in an old-fashioned schoolmaster's mortar-board, encircled by heads of Beatles, Cilla, Billy J and all his other Mersey Beat protégés like one big happy kindergarten.

We were all quite contentedly resigned to no interview when Paul McCartney suddenly walked past, in jeans and black polo neck, holding a packet of Juicy Fruit gum. 'I know that face', somebody said wanly, at which he paused and grinned. 'Can we come in and talk to you?' I asked. 'Sure,' he replied. And suddenly there we were, talking to them.

They had been allotted a kind of subterranean 'green room', with 1930s brocade sofas and armchairs, and opaque French doors covering one entire wall. Municipal waitresses, in black uniforms and white aprons, were clearing away their half-eaten supper of steak and trifle. The only light came from varnished standard lamps and a blue TV screen, showing an episode of The Avengers with Diana Rigg and Patrick Mcnee. Near it in the twilight floated George Harrison's pale, unhappy face.

Two more faces floated up to talk to us - Ringo's and John's. Both were instantly friendly and nice. You would have thought it the first time they had ever been interviewed by stammering local reporters. Ringo sat in a brocade armchair, with John perched on its arm. McCartney came and went hyperactively, chewing Juicy Fruit. Only George remained apart and glum on his distant sofa, watching The Avengers.

Our questions were, of course, stupendously banal. 'What's your favourite television programme?' 'Do you prefer BBC or ITV?' I asked John why, as I had read, he no longer ended their stage performance with Twist and Shout. 'We'd done it so many times,' he replied. 'It was starting to sicken us...' I asked McCartney about his 'violin bass', now copied by so many other groups. 'I like 'em because they're cheap,' he said. 'Only fifty-two guineas. I'm skinflint, you see. And they're nice and light. Here - try it.' With that he tossed the bass over to me.

I cannot overstress the phenomenon of this niceness and friendliness. Compare it to the scene in *Don't Look Back*, Don Pennebaker's film of that same year, where a hapless reporter in Birmingham or Manchester is mercilessly taken apart by the young Bob Dylan. The Beatles had even less reason to be nice to nobodies - but they were. I asked if we could stay and talk to them a little longer. 'Sure,' the three of them agreed. Then Neil Aspinall, their road manager, came over and curtly ordered us to leave. 'But they said we could stay,' I protested. 'Well, I say you've got to go,' he snapped.

Afterwards, we stood backstage and listened to their performance. One could hear nothing but girls screaming and screaming on an eerie, continuous note like the ceremonial whistles when naval captains come aboard warships. A luckier colleague who made it into the wings reported that, during one totally unheard number, John had crashed his arm in fury over the keys of his Vox organ.

★

A few weeks later, my grainy monochrome life burst into VistAvision and Cinemascope. I was offered a job as feature-writer with *The Sunday Times Magazine*, trendiest of Britain's new 'colour supplements'. One day, I was in drab old Newcastle, covering inquests, courts and industrial tribunals. The next, I was down in London, roaring towards Soho in Gerald Scarfe's E-Type, a mini-skirted girl on my lap. The Sixties had hauled me aboard at last.

No memoir of Swinging London and Pop culture in that era can omit *The Sunday Times Magazine*. As powerfully as King's Road or Carnaby Street, its pages defined the new world, so unexpected by Socialist Britain, where glamour and fashion and trivia ruled, and youth was everything. Each Sunday's issue was as eagerly awaited as some new LP, with its photographs of Jean Shrimpton by David Bailey, its pages of Quant-cropped models in white Courrèges boots, its artwork by David Hockney and Peter Blake, its scarcely less compulsive glossy ads for double cream, fluffy Kosset carpets and After Eight mints. For constant innovation and surprise allied to incalculable glamour it had no rival in any medium - except, of course, The Beatles.

Oddly enough, Pop music received almost no coverage in its pages. What little there was lay under the firm control of the deputy editor, Derek Jewell, a man in his late thir-

ties. One day when I arrived at the 'ideas lunch' that was such a regular and pleasant feature of editorial life, he was brandishing a copy of The Beatles' new album, *Revolver*. It had a black and white cover illustration, like something our own art director might have commissioned. 'The Beatles,' Derek Jewell said, 'are the greatest celebrants of modern urban life since The Beach Boys'.

Though my *Sunday Times* assignments were wondrously exciting, they had little to do with Pop music and nothing to do with The Beatles. Too many people already had the subject too well tied down. There was Derek Jewell in our paper, Tony Palmer in *The Observer*, Geoffrey Cannon in *The Guardian*, William Mann in *The Times*, all vying to define them as 'celebrants of modern urban life' or 'the greatest writers of popular songs since Schubert'. Above all there was the London *Evening Standard* whose columnists Maureen Cleave and Ray Connolly almost seemed to cohabit with them. I was no nearer than *Standard* newsvendors to the great Beatle news stories of '66 and '67: the furore over John's 'bigger than Jesus' remark (originally to Maureen Cleave); the subsequent moral backlash in America, with Beatles albums cast onto St Joan-style bonfires, and death threats made on-camera by hooded Grand Wizards of the Ku Klux Klan; the roughing-up at Manila airport after their supposed insult to Imelda Marcos; the final concert at Candlestick Park, San Francisco, ending a saga that seemed to have lasted a thousand years though, in fact, it had lasted barely three. I wrote not a word about any of these

events. There were too many already on the bandwagon.

The Beatles second flowering as a 'studio group' was to me just background noise on assignments the length and breadth of England. Yellow Submarine reminds me of The Shetland Isles during the Viking fire festival, Up Helly-aa. Penny Lane reminds me of interviewing the speed ace Donald Campbell, a few days before his powerboat Bluebird fatally broke up on Coniston Water. *Sgt. Pepper's Lonely Hearts Club Band* reminds me of driving to interview Diana Dors in an open MGB with a photographer who really did say 'Love and peace'. The opening track was playing as we sat around the sex goddess's swimming pool with her little dogs and her two kaftaned boyfriends. I can see that spun-platinum hair; those great red, bee-stung lips singing 'Sergeant Pepper's Lonely...Sergeant Pepper's Lonely...'

John Lennon's increasing rebellion and recalcitrance, and his obvious power to influence the other three, filled me with the same dismay as everyone else. It was as if a soft toy one liked to cuddle had suddenly developed sharp corners that could cut, and extruded wires that could put one's eye out. I resented him for changing neat, happy little songs into eerie, complicated ones; for remodelling the perfect Fab Four prototype into wilder and wilder asymmetry. I didn't want The Beatles to put on granny-specs, grow moustaches, wear hippy chains and smocks and become followers of the Maharishi. I wanted them still in brand-new button-downs or polo-necks, clowning on Juke Box Jury, then going off to some great party.

His affair with Yoko Ono seemed the ultimate perversity. Why a funny-looking Japanese woman when there must be so many beautiful, willing girls? Yoko was already a figure of fun, lampooned in *The Sunday Times'* 'Atticus' column for making a film about bare bottoms. The 'Atticus' columnist, Hunter Davies, went on to write a piece about Paul McCartney, and establish a strong rapport. As a result, he was commissioned to write The Beatles' authorised biography. I remember him walking round the office with page proofs of a spin-off article about their new film, *Magical Mystery Tour*.

I felt no twinge of envy or competitiveness. I was still at the very back of the crowd.

★

The notion that I might write something about The Beatles finally came in August, 1969. It was not my idea, but one pressed on me by my friend Dick Adler, who had just become editor of the American entertainment magazine *Show*. 'I'd love to have a piece about all the stuff that's going on with Apple,' he said. 'Why not go down there and hang around for a couple of weeks? And see if you can get the four of them photographed as directors sitting round a boardroom table.'

Even for this late story it seemed horribly late in the day. The Beatles' Apple venture had been running a year already, generating millions of words in the British and international press. How they wanted to create a business organisation that would give young talent and enterprise the early backing which they themselves had lacked. How the vast Beatle fortunes would be used to subsidise, not only would-be musicians but also would-be painters, sculptors, novelists, poets, inventors and architects. How, in a short time, the utopian ideal seemed to have dissolved in a welter of wound-up divisions and shut-down boutiques, the four business Beatles themselves reportedly at personal loggerheads. How, in an apparently terminal phase, the Rolling Stones' former manager Allen Klein had been brought in to wield the axe.

And, running parallel with the Apple saga, the personal saga of John Lennon himself, a figure weirdly torn between corporate businessman, long-haired fakir and public clown. One could by now base an entire journalistic career on following Yoko and him through the unending cycle of their stunts and outrages: the 'bed-ins', the 'bag-ins', the drug-busts, the public nudity. The *Daily Mirror* spoke for all in mourning 'a not inconsiderable talent who seems to have gone totally off his rocker'.

As well as cohorts of Pop journalists in every language, The Beatles were now covered by financial journalists, property journalists, investigative journalists. *The Sunday Times*' 'Insight' team, at that same moment was working on a detailed dissection of Allen Klein's business affairs. There seemed less room than ever on the bandwagon. Nevertheless, I forced myself to call the Apple Press Office.

'I've been asked to do a piece about you by American *Show* magazine,' I said to the girl who answered. 'I'd like to come in and just hang around.'

'Okay,' she said. 'Come in and just hang around.'

To find The Beatles in London, you turned left off Regent Street, through the winding crevice of Mayfair that contains Gieves & Hawkes, Blades boutique and the Albany Cigarette Co. Then sharp right into Savile Row, a double row of bespoke tailoring establishments behind gold-lettered plate glass windows raised above the street. Only two doors along on your right was the Georgian house, perfect in every detail but the bedraggled groups of girls eternally haunting its front step.

Despite the presence of a frock-coated doorman, getting inside was ridiculously easy. You stated your business to a solitary receptionist and, after the briefest intercom exchange, were bidden to 'go on up'. On the staircase wall hung an oil painting of honey-coloured lion cubs that seemed to symbolise the house's owners as the world still imagined them: invincibly young, beautiful and strong, romping and rolling together in perpetual play.

The only serious vetting I had to undergo was by Derek Taylor, The Beatles' personal press officer, a figure in his own way almost as sought after. Slim and moustachioed like some 1930s Tango champion, Taylor ruled the second floor Press Office where journalists, and every other type of freeloader, could spend whole days if they wished, drinking The Beatles' Scotch and Coke, smoking The Beatles' Benson & Hedges Gold, eating The Beatles' food, which Cordon Bleu cooks prepared in an adjacent kitchen. Most, indeed, went there to see Taylor rather than for any new Fab Four intelligence. He had a way of talking that was all his own: quiet, funny, scurrilously indiscreet about his employers' affairs, as well as unshakably loyal.

On the basis of no music journalism – but, rather, an article I'd written about Charles Atlas the strong man – Derek Taylor said I could stay around Apple, observing The Beatles at business. The difficulty was not every Beatle came there regularly any more. I mentioned the idea of photographing

all four together round a boardroom table, at which Taylor sharply drew in his breath. One might have been *Life* magazine in World War II, asking Buckingham Palace for permission to photograph George VI in his bath.

The rift, I quickly learned, was far worse that anyone knew, or wanted to know. Since Allen Klein's appointment as manager by a majority vote; Paul McCartney had withdrawn in disgust to his Scottish farm with his new wife, Linda. George and Ringo now came in to Apple sporadically and with dwindling interest. The only one still there on anything like a day-to-day basis was John.

Derek Taylor took me down to his office the very next day. The slightly idiotic thing was that, under my 'fly-on-the-wall' brief from *Show* magazine, I was not going to interview him. I was merely to sit and watch other people interview him.

The room was on the ground floor at the front, symbolically close to Savile Row with its ever-present gawpers and the knot of girls by the step. Just inside the door, like a butler or major-domo, stood one of the perspex robots from the recently-unveiled Plastic Ono Band. The panelled walls were festooned with placards in familiar Lennon script, mixing polemic and pun – 'Bed Peace', 'Bag Peace', 'Hair Peace', 'Peace Off'. In the eighteenth century fireplace, a nude plastic doll had been

stood on its head as if to demonstrate some advanced technique from the *Kama Sutra*. Below the double casement was a wide white desk, littered with books, newspapers, files, Magic Markers, plates of half-eaten brown rice and chocolate cake; and behind this sat John with Yoko.

It's hard to credit how unrecognisable he looked in those days, with his apostle-length hair and bushy beard and the little round glasses through which he could stare with the fixedness of some mad Russian monk. But the voice that came through the beard was as deep and sane as ever, no matter what he happened to be saying. The Gauloises cigarettes he chain-smoked added another reassuring secular touch. Yoko sat on his right in a purple shift, picking at something on a plate with a long spoon, post-scripting all his sentences in her odd little flat chirrup. Also present was their joint personal assistant and 'art adviser', a washed-out Medusa of a young man named Anthony Fawcett.

It was, for then, a fairly ordinary day of John and Yoko news. The previous night, they had been at the Institute of Contemporary Arts, showing the film of John's penis in close-up. They were shortly to launch a campaign on behalf of James Hanratty, an Irishman hanged in the early Sixties – many believed unjustly – for an horrific murder on the A6. Reverberations still continued of John's recent statement to *Disc and Music Echo* that he was 'almost broke', at least down to his 'last fifty thousand pounds'. Plus, of course, the perennial front page stories; what The Beatles were doing; what Apple was doing; what, in the name of goodness, John Lennon thought he was doing.

He explained it exactly and clearly, through that straggled beard, to a dozen or more different visitors. He was turning the tables on the media that had so long hounded him as a Beatle; exploiting press and TV, as they had exploited him, to announce his new life, new conscience and new causes. 'The Blue Meanies, or whatever they are, still preach violence all the time in every newspaper, every TV show and every magazine. The least Yoko and I can do is hog the headlines and make people laugh. We're quite willing to be the world's clowns if it will do any good. For reasons known only to themselves, people print what I say. So I say "Peace".'

Every journalist who came in that afternoon was offered a Gauloise, and went away with a first class John Lennon quote. On his supposed 'poverty': 'I haven't had any income for about two years. It's been all bloody outcome.' On the rationalisation of Apple 'The circus has left town, but we still own the site.' On the liberating effect of performance art: 'We're all a lot of frozen jellies. It just needs someone to turn off the fridge.' Rather than the cynical predator she was generally supposed, Yoko seemed shy, even naive, as when one reporter asked what critical response there had

been to the film of John's penis. 'The critics wouldn't touch it,' Yoko replied.

My own conceit and arrogance on this occasion were fairly disgusting. As a *Sunday Times Magazine* person, albeit moonlighting for *Show*, I felt far above the ruck of everyday journalism, and so entitled to punctuate the different interviews with supposedly bright and original comments of my own. It was behaviour richly deserving the ammoniac scorn which John reserved for any poseur or pseud. The mad monk face listened to me intently, but for some reason the annihilating put-down never came. Just after one of my more fatuous digressions, Derek Taylor came in to say the interviewer's time had run out. 'No, hold on...' John said, as the man obediently rose. 'He hasn't had his proper crack of the whip yet...'

Though I spent several weeks more at Apple, no comparable encounters with other Beatles came my way. Mostly I sat in the Press Office next to Derek Taylor's scalloped wickerwork chair, listening to Taylor on the phone in service of John and Yoko. Trying to arrange a private plane to take them to the Toronto Rock Festival. Trying to find four acorns which they could bury as a gesture for world peace. Trying to secure John's re-entry into America after his 'crime of moral turpitude', as US Immigration

termed the recent drug-bust. Trying to find Yoko's daughter, Kyoko, and a long-out-of-print book entitled *Queer Things About Japan*.

I noticed the general sniping and bitchery about them, in which only Derek Taylor forbore to join. Neil Aspinall, the ex-roadie, one day remarked on the prevailing fashion for beards. 'Everyone seems to have them now - John, George, Ringo, and Yoko's trying...' In my only encounter with George and Ringo, even they were sending John up over his plan to get to Toronto and play at the rock festival all inside one weekend. 'D'you fancy going to Australia to play?' George sarcastically asked Ringo. 'We get back tomorrow.'

The penultimate Beatles album had now been released, and played all day through the Press Office loudspeakers. Whenever I hear *Abbey Road* now, I see that high-ceilinged Georgian room with its potted plants and fun sculptures, its bespeckled, wriggling light-show, its palpable atmosphere of drift and dread. The whole album was nothing more nor less than an extended boardroom row, John's directorial voice warring with Paul McCartney's over policy beyond resolution. Paul had captured the middle ground for the middle-of-the-road, but John held the start and finish, from the voodoo hiss of Come Together to those final jotted fragments about Polythene Pam and Mean Mr Mustard. Each time the album ended and began again, the same thought came: it's over.

Paul was the one who seemed to bear all the hurt of the final break, singing Let It Be with such regret in his great brown eyes. From John came only the infuriated relief of a lifer whose parole has finally come through. 'Think about it,' he urged one reporter, his voice curdled with contempt. 'It's just a rock band breakin' up, like they often do. It's not the end of the bloody world.'

The initial feeling, indeed, was of gain as much as loss. From a group that had lost its way, four separate talents emerged to follow paths of multifarious promise. There was genuine pleasure in George Harrison's final recognition as a performer and sensibility in his own right, with his album, *All Things Must Pass*, and his impressive Concert for Bangladesh. Even Ringo Starr, that great bit-part player, enjoyed a succession of hit albums and singles, his cheery honk augmented by Harrison, Eric Clapton and the cream of international studio talent.

For the sundered components Lennon and McCartney, things seemed to have turned out best of all. Paul was free at last to write his sticky ballads without John's cynical editorial eye over his shoulder. John was free to say and be what he liked without Paul fussily picking fluff off his lapel. This should have been a brilliant time for him yet, somehow, it wasn't. One pictures him at the time of Imagine, alone with Yoko in that preposterous

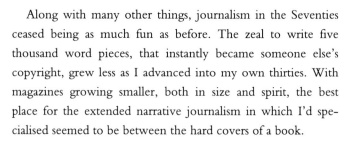

stately home called Tittenhurst Park; two ragged Ben Gunn figures, marooned amid terrible, endless seas of parquet and white.

Then, suddenly, he was gone: fled away to New York, and a new life of dwindling achievement and declining charm. He continued to make music, which his admirers increasingly had to force themselves to like. Every year or so, a rumour of a Beatles reunion would begin to circulate, and that same curdled voice would be audible from Manhattan, remorselessly puncturing it. He had disappeared into a foreign culture - Green Cards, *The Village Voice*, The Dick Cavett Show - from which blurred and fragmented reports came back. How he had left Yoko, and drunkenly made a public fool of himself. How he had returned to Yoko, fathered another child and decided to stay at home more. He and the decade seemed to be describing an almost symbiotic downward curve.

Along with many other things, journalism in the Seventies ceased being as much fun as before. The zeal to write five thousand word pieces, that instantly became someone else's copyright, grew less as I advanced into my own thirties. With magazines growing smaller, both in size and spirit, the best place for the extended narrative journalism in which I'd specialised seemed to be between the hard covers of a book.

In late 1978, I was discussing with some friends which biographical subject would command the largest, most avid readership throughout the world. Something made me suddenly blurt out 'The Beatles'.

The response was unanimously negative. 'Everyone knows that story...it's been told so many times...Anyway, lots of other groups since have been far bigger than The Beatles...Abba have outsold them dozens of times...And the punks hate them...It's only Sixties nostalgics like you who still play their music...A lot of young people today don't even know who they were...'

A few days later, I was riding in a car with a friend's five year-old son. I asked what was his favourite record. In answer, he began to sing, beating time on the car seat. 'You say you wanna revo-lu-sh-ah-an, we-e-ell you know...'

★

My aims and expectations at the start were equally modest. To take a subject hitherto regarded as the exclusive preserve of fan mags and pulp picturebooks, and apply grown-up journalistic techniques: investigation, analysis and objective narrative prose. To discard the story everyone insisted they knew, and re-research it from the very start, believing nothing already written or stored in newspaper files. To try to give the well-known scenes and tableaux a fresh slant by adding historical perspective. To try to recreate the sound and feel of Beatles music and Beatle times. In early 1979, I could persuade almost no one it wasn't the worst possible idea. I grew so self-conscious, I'd try to avoid even mentioning the name 'Beatles'. I said I was writing a book on popular culture in the Sixties.

The first discovery was that the four subjects themselves

would not be accessible. Nowadays, Paul, George and Ringo talk freely about life as a Beatle; then, in lingering aftershock, they could not bear even to think about it. The only hope was John Lennon, exiled in New York. I wrote to him at the Dakota building, and got a form letter from an assistant at 'Studio One', thanking me for my interest, but saying John and Yoko were too busy with their projects to do interviews at present. I resolved to keep trying. Meantime, I would treat the four Beatles as characters in an epic nonfiction novel, the title of which now came to me: *Shout*.

I began with the most visible and obvious background names: George Martin, their record producer; Dick James, their music publisher; Maureen Cleave, who wrote all those *Evening Standard* columns about them; Brian Matthew, who introduced them on all those radio and TV shows. I also had the inestimable luck to meet Mark Lewisohn, a twenty-one-year-old BBC clerk, recently dubbed 'Beatle Brain of Britain', who, in addition to encyclopedic knowledge, possessed a cache of their records, both official and 'bootleg', their monthly magazine and the special souvenir discs they would record specially for their fan club each Christmas.

The interviews were about The Beatles. But the quotable bits, almost always, were about John Lennon. To George Martin, in the early days, he was like a precocious child, only half-aware of the joltingly funny things he said. Offered his first taste of mange-tout peas in a restaurant, he said, 'OK - but put them over there, not near the food'. Maureen Cleave remembered her surprise on meeting a Pop star whose hero was William, Richmal Crompton's lawless eleven-year-old. Brian Matthew remembered interviewing The Beatles on radio just after his return from holiday in Spain. As the schoolmasterly compere framed a first question, John leaned and said into the microphone, 'Brian's nose is peeling, folks'.

I heard him, too, speaking to Beatles fans on their 1964 Christmas disc, reading out the banalities of some PRO with deadpan irony. 'Gosh, what a lot's happened since we spoke to you last...All of us wish all of you a very, very happy Chrimble and a gear New Year...' His voice, from the deepest blizzards of Beatlemania, sending the whole thing up rotten.

After a few weeks, my expectations had dramatically changed. I felt like someone who had wandered on to an archaeological site where, supposedly, everything interesting had long ago been excavated, examined, labelled and put on show. Yet the first tentative prod of my trowel turned up gold. And from there, a whole lost city revealed itself.

The Beatles story that everyone knew so well turned out to be but the tiniest fraction of the complete one. Between the landmark events, engraved on millions of minds, whole seams of wonderful stuff lay untapped. How had it all been missed by that huge journalistic bandwagon? Chiefly, I discovered, because reporters covering The Beatles in the Sixties worked to a predetermined formula. They wrote, not what they saw but what their besotted audience wanted to hear. The dilemma was explained by Bob Hart, a columnist for *The Sun* in its last days as a reasonable tabloid. 'In every Beatles piece, you knew the line you had to take. It wasn't real people; it was cuddly moptops. You knew that if you didn't do it that way, the *Mirror* would, the *Express* would and the *Mail* would. You were writing in self-defence.'

The field I had always believed ridiculously overcrowded now proved to contain only myself. The one other serious book, Hunter Davies's authorised biography, stopped in 1968, before the White Album, Yoko, Apple and Allen Klein. And being 'authorised' meant censorship of important facts - notably that Brian Epstein was homosexual, and that what motivated his crazy, hopeless, brilliant management of The Beatles above all was being in love with John.

That I could not talk directly to John, Paul, George and Ringo quickly ceased to matter. For it had become plain that, for much of their career, The Beatles themselves had no idea what was going on around them. One could not ask them about the ghastly dip in America's self-esteem after the Kennedy assassination, which made her receptive to British Pop music for the first time ever. Nor about the small-scale hype which produced those famous scenes at JFK Airport. Nor about the laughable knockdown fee they got for appearing on The Ed Sullivan Show. Nor about Epstein's disastrous merchandising deals in the US, which allowed millions of dollars to blow away. During this period, I heard Paul McCartney say on radio that their conquest of America had been 'all planned down to the last detail'. I realised that the ultimate victims of Beatle mythology were The Beatles.

The real story was one of stupendous natural talent, but also stupendous luck; absurdly chain-reacting chapters of accidents between Liverpool, Hamburg, London and New York. It was a classic instance of human beings moving towards the right goal by every conceivable wrong turning and digression. It was a run of odds constantly paying off at a million to one - for instance, how a young northern shopkeeper with a nervous blush happened to take his discovery first to a Fifties crooner-turned-song-publisher, then to an

obscure producer of comedy records with EMI. That, for me, still remains the most amazing Beatle fact of all. The greatest show business phenomenon in history was run by three honest men.

The real story had least of all to do with my own envious button-down dream, years earlier on The County Newspaper for Huntingdonshire. To talk to people with them backstage, at Juke Box Jury or The Ed Sullivan Show, was to see their life, no longer as everlasting joy and fun but as an Edgar Allan Poe nightmare. To be walled up in dressing-rooms, buried under screams. To travel the world, yet see nothing. To move never slower than a run for your life. To be so trapped, bombarded and gouged by mindless adoration, you could start to feel you were ageing at twice the normal rate...

I remembered John Lennon's bitter refusal even to con-template playing with the other three again. 'Why should the Beatles give more? Didn't they give everything on God's Earth for ten years? Didn't they give *themselves*?' I began to see what it was he had so long and furiously tried to escape.

Liverpool was where it all began. And in Liverpool, this implausible journey ends. I had meant to go there on a week's research trip that would cover everything. I stayed a month, then found myself returning again and again.

No comprehension - or, I think, real enjoyment - of The Beatles is possible without first understanding Liverpool. You must understand a city almost Athenian in the grandeur of its colonnades, temples and squares. You must understand the broad river, criss-crossed by white ferries, where great liners once docked, blowing ashore the newest, jazziest rumours from New York. You must understand the impossible pomp of the Adelphi Hotel; the fearsome back-to-back slums of Toxteth and Garston; the over-compensatingly respectable golf club suburbs of Woolton, Allerton and Childwall. You must understand the population, so richly plundered from nearby Wales and Ireland, as well as China and Africa, and its celebrated humour, most usually expressed in types of baroque insult. When a Liverpudlian tells someone they're useless, he says they are 'as useful as a one-legged man in an arse-kicking contest'.

You must also understand the ache of a supremely confident Victorian past in a present laid waste by unemployment, recession and almost vindictive 'redevelopment'. It was going on even before The Beatles went away. John Lennon's most personal song, In My Life, was not about friends so much as the lost city landmarks of his 1950s childhood. An unfinished verse mourns 'The Dockers' Umbrella', as they called the elevated railway that once ran above the whole teeming river-front.

I visited the places from Beatle folklore, now more famous worldwide than St George's Hall or the Liver Insurance building. The brief street of shops called Penny Lane whose nameplate never withstands souvenir-hunters longer than a few days. The grim-looking Salvation Army home on what used to be Strawberry Field. The cobbled alleyway among grain and banana warehouses where The Cavern Club lay buried. The electrical shop in neighbouring Whitechapel, from which Brian Epstein was finally lured forth. It was by then a Rumbelow's discount store, tiled in grimy polystyrene. But beyond the flimsy partition one could still glimpse the tasteful collage of LP sleeves with which Brian decorated the original ceiling, before his eye was spectacularly diverted from mere shopkeeping.

In ornate nineteenth century pubs or modern cellar dives I talked to those whom the whirlwind had left behind. To Allan Williams, The Beatles' first manager, who drove them to Hamburg in a van with his Chinese wife, Beryl, and a West Indian named Lord Woodbine. To Bob Wooler, the erudite Cavern disc jockey who lent them rare American R & B singles to plagiarise, like Chan Romero's Hippy Hippy Shake. To Pete Best, the fatally good-looking drummer, sacked and replaced by Ringo on the very eve of the breakthrough. I grew used to 'Liverpool eyes'; that common look of fathomless disappointment and mystification at having missed the pots and pots of gold.

★

My black and red Chinese notebooks, from Lewis's department store, filled with dozens of unheard or incomplete anecdotes in the story that everyone 'knew'. How Paul McCartney's mother had been a local authority midwife (Mother Mary) and George Harrison's grandmother, a lamp-lighter. How Ritchie Starkey, alias Ringo Starr, had spent almost his entire childhood in hospital. How, when Brian Epstein approached a local photographer to take shots of his 'group', the photographer thought he meant a wedding group. How Brian, at the start, made comical efforts to impress The Beatles with his managerial clout, even having himself called to the phone in Birkenhead pubs to take fictitious calls from Elvis Presley's manager, Colonel Tom Parker.

When one writes a biography there are some parts which

one must work to animate, but others which live and breathe on their own. For me, as I strove to keep four main characters simultaneously functioning, the parts of the book which always instantly lived and breathed were those about John.

I could sometimes almost feel I had grown up and knocked around with the dour, vague, hilarious, irascible, unreliable youth whose face always mocked, even from the mildewed stage of The Cavern Club. The youth who, just as often, would be photographed with face and limbs contorted in cruel burlesque of a spastic child. The youth who hated to wear his horn-rimmed glasses, and whose myopic literary gift, long before being applied to songs, used to come out in a little local music paper called *Mersey Beat*. 'Many people ask, what are Beatles? Why Beatles? Ugh, Beatles, how did the name arrive? So we will tell you. It came in a vision - a man appeared on a flaming pie and said unto them "From this day on, you are Beatles" "Thank you, Mister Man," they said, thanking him...'

The portrait was not all sweetness, and certainly not all light. My most revealing contact was Brian Epstein's ex-lover Joe Flannery, a gentle, paternal man whose house The Beatles would use as base-camp between their Merseyside gigs. In a peck-order already well established, John would sleep on the couch, leaving Paul to push two armchairs together.

From Joe Flannery I heard of his darker side: his ruthless despotism over weaker souls, like Brian Epstein, and his first wife, Cynthia; his fecklessness, cruelty and occasional mad truculence. There also were tales of drink and pill orgies on the Hamburg Reeperbahn that had taken all Epstein's skill in news-management to suppress. The point was, though, that unlike Paul, John never attempted to hide this uglier face. His most constant plea was for recognition as a human being, light and shade. 'People always try and put me in their bag,' I remembered him saying. 'They want me to be lovable, but I never was that. I was always just "Lennon".'

More than a counterweight was the warmth of his friendship, especially with Stu Sutcliffe, 'the fifth Beatle', whose death from a brain haemorrhage tragically ended a brilliant painting career. I visited the Liverpool student pub, weirdly called Ye Cracke, and the site of the Jacaranda coffee bar, in either of which they would sit for hour after hour, hatching sub-Kerouac fantasies. I also saw a photograph of them on the beach in Germany, Sutcliffe making a collage with John an eager assistant. I realised how, for the rest of his life, he had been looking for leaders, gurus; someone to make him dare.

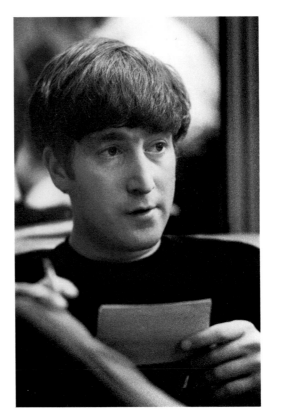

It was through these fierce platonic male friendships - with Stu Sutcliffe, with his school crony Pete Shotton and ultimately with Paul McCartney - that I came closest to understanding him in all his contradictions and paradox. Brilliant, hilarious and inspired, but also indolent and vague. Rebellious and anarchic, but also self-doubting and cautious. Ruthless, exploitative, sometimes unspeakably callous and vicious, but also considerate, decent and kind. A hero whose abiding propensity turned out to be hero-worship. Of Van Gogh even more than Chuck Berry. Of swaggering waterfront Teddy Boys and, later, a Japanese woman with the chutzpah to put an apple on show in an art-gallery, with a fifty pound price tag attached to it.

There was always an odd separation in my mind between the John Lennon of those almost sepia Victorian Liverpool days and the John Lennon of now, 'somewhere in New York City'. I had decided my narrative would end in 1970, with the simultaneous end of the Beatles and the Sixties. I had little interest in his subse-quent lost decade, wherein the greatest loss seemed that of articulateness and humour. I did stumble on one great relevant truth: that Liverpool and New York are very much alike. They have the same great waterfront buildings, the same piers and wharves, the same muddy river, polyglot peoples and salty wit. Standing at the Pier Head, looking out to Liverpool Bay and the North Atlantic beyond, I would remember how he, too, would stand here and think that 'the next place you come to is America'.

I saw the Victorian art college in Hope Street, where he spent three hopeless, unmotivated years. I met Arthur Ballard, the teacher who tried to make him use his talent for caricature. Mostly, Ballard remembered him and a half-Arab boy named Jeff Mohammed, getting drunk and peeing into lift-shafts. But also the time he was found alone, crying on the big staircase window-sill. His mother had been killed by a speeding motorist, a few days before.

I went to his old school, Quarry Bank, and saw the multiplicity of crimes for which his name appeared in its 1956 punishment book. 'Cutting class and going awol.' 'Gambling on school field during House match.' 'Throwing blackboard duster out of window.' That same hazy summer afternoon, I walked through Woolton village to the site of the church garden fête where he and Paul McCartney met. I could almost fancy I heard the sounds of that festive Saturday afternoon: the brass bands, hoop-la and sheepdog-trials, the first collision of their voices, against tinny little acoustic guitars.

Another day, far from Liverpool, I talked to Mimi Smith, the aunt who brought him up; a lean, shrewd woman, always his match and more. I saw the spotless suburban home, with firm rules about washing 'face, hands and knees'. I could visualise the eleven-year-old, in his baggy grey flannel shorts with an S-clasp school belt.

The kind of boy who, at one moment, would give you a Chinese burn, at the next fling his arm affectionately round your neck. The boy whose first dream of all was to be Just William.

Aunt Mimi told me that the last time he had rung her from New York, they had had a row, she had shouted 'Damn you, Lennon!' and slammed the receiver down. A few moments later, the phone had rung again. John's voice had come across the hemispheres, contritely as of old. 'You're not still cross with me, Mimi, are you?'

★

Late in 1980, as I was finishing the book, his voice came back on the radio. By pure, irrelevant chance I once again happened to be in a bathroom. My first reaction was 'That can't be John Lennon', for it sounded just too ridiculously like him. The song, (Just Like) Starting Over, had a Phil Spector-ish-Goffin-King feel, like a Beatles B-side circa 1964. All it lacked was what I had concluded he would always fatally lack - Paul McCartney's voice to sweeten and tauten the harmony.

What one noticed was not the song, but the quality in ·the voice. That sandpaper rasp, once likened by George Martin to 'tearing flesh', had softened and relaxed at last. 'Our love is still special' ran one of the lines. By whatever strange route, the end result of Yoko had been to produce stability and mature happiness.

He was all over the radio then, as well as *Newsweek* and *Playboy* magazines, talking about *Double Fantasy*, his first album for five years, and his intervening time as 'househusband', looking after his son Sean, doing housework, learning to bake bread. His style of narrative was, as ever, unique. 'When I baked my first loaf, I looked at it and said "Don't I get a Gold Record now?"' One's smile joined up with other smiles all the way back to the 1963 Royal Command Performance. Photographs, released at the same time, put an end to rumours that he'd gone bald and that cocaine had rotted away his nose. He had returned from his lost decade looking slim, healthy, almost better than the teenager he had started out. It was a fitting reward for someone who had always so eschewed personal conceit and public facade; whose great gift to unreal times had been his indestructible authenticity. And who seemed to have come through all his eras of madness, sane to the very last.

Even though my manuscript was now complete and delivered to the publisher, I still hoped the wave of *Double Fantasy* media promotion would get me across to New York to interview him, if nothing else for some form of postscript. That hope was shattered by a phone call in the early hours of December 9, from a friend in New York I had not spoken to for some years. She told me that John Lennon had just been shot by an unidentified young man outside the Dakota Building. John Lennon was dead.

For the present, I had no time for any personal reaction. Right at the front of the crowd now, I had to go through all my two years' research again and produce a three-thousand-word obituary for *The Sunday Times*. I little imagined that in a few weeks' time, by the same irony that has governed this whole account, I would be inside the Dakota Building, examining his old Beatle suits, his Quarry Bank school cap and his gold Egyptian mummy. Looking into every room of the huge white apartment over Central Park where he had thought he would be left alone at last.

While I worked, friends rang me continually, as friends were ringing one another all over the world. No other death ever moved such millions to need for contact and mutual comfort. One friend summed up the feeling, not articulately but exactly. 'It's the first time they've killed anyone like that.'

In the background, the TV screen murmured with panoramic shock and disbelief. 'I can't believe he's dead,' said a teenage boy in New York. ' He kept me from dying so many times.' I could not in all honesty say he had kept me from dying. I could say he had kept a down-at-heel beginner journalist, in those pre-historic early Sixties, from wanting to crawl into his own wallet and hide.

When the three-thousand-word obituary was done, I dictated the whole thing over the phone to a *Sunday Times* copytaker. I felt nothing until its last line - the one spoken by that anxious voice from New York to his aunt.

'You're not still cross with me, Mimi, are you?'

I put the telephone down, then felt myself begin to cry.

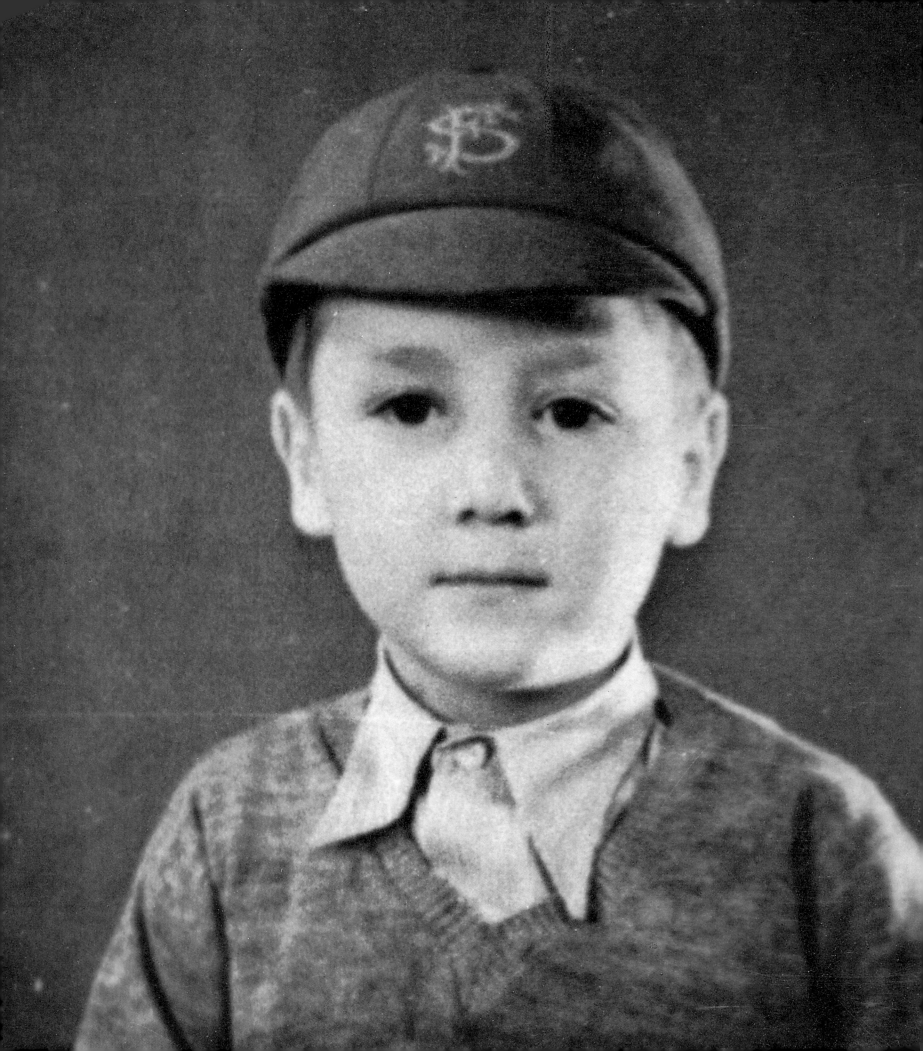

John Winston Lennon.

Born October 9, 1940, Oxford Road Maternity Hospital, Liverpool.

Father, Alfred 'Freddy' Lennon, itinerant ship's steward. Mother, Julia, née Stanley.

Both amateur entertainers, Freddy a singer of romantic songs,

Julia (above) proficient on banjo. Neither one a scrupulous or selfless parent.

After a brief tug-of-war between Freddy and Julia, John is handed over to be raised by his childless Aunt Mary – Mimi. He grows up in Mimi's house, 'Mendips', a neat semi-detached villa in Menlove Avenue, Woolton, Liverpool.

Mimi is brisk and strong-willed, but devoted to her charge.

'All through his childhood, there was never a night when I set foot out of that house. I'd stand at the bottom of the stairs and hear him singing to himself.'

A Treasury of Art and Poetry

This book contains only the work of J.W. Lennon, with additional work by J.W. Lennon, and a helping hand given by J.W. Lennon, not forgetting J.W. Lennon. Who is this J.W. Lennon?
Here are some remark by a few famous Newspapers.

"A good book better" — J.W. Lennon of the Daily Howl
"This book has many good uses and should go down well" — The Sanitory Journal
"Yes" — Fred Emney Fan Club Magazine
"(Belch!)" — Garston Herald.

"And then there's the one about the Bishop and the actress....."

Schools: Dovedale
Primary, near Penny Lane,
then Quarry Bank High
School (sometimes called
'The Eton of the Labour
Party').

An incorrigible truant and
troublemaker, repeatedly
punished by caning,
detention, even temporary
expulsion. Only interested
in reading, and writing
and illustrating stories.
Chronically bad eyesight
fosters private language of
puns and Goonish
wordplay. His role model
is Just William, Richmal
Crompton's mischievous
but hilarious 11 year-old.
'Whenever the phone
went at 11 in the
morning,' Aunt Mimi
says, 'I'd know it was the
school office. I'd think
"Oh Lord, what's he done
now?"'

'Without Elvis there would have been no Beatles.'

Aged 15, becomes besotted by the first wave of American Rock 'n' Roll Music, Bill Haley, Little Richard, Eddie Cochran, especially the sublime young punk Elvis Presley singing Heartbreak Hotel. Simultaneous British vogue for homespun folk or 'skiffle' music – spearheaded by Lonnie Donegan – leads him to take up guitar.

'He stood out in that porch practising for so many hours, I think he wore away the brickwork with his behind.'

'I said "The guitar's all very well, John, but you'll never make a living out of it." '

July 6, 1957. John's Quarry Men skiffle group perform at Woolton Parish Church garden fête. A mutual friend, Ivan Vaughan, brings along 15 year-old Paul McCartney, who auditions by playing Eddie Cochran's Twenty Flight Rock.

John and Paul could not be more different - one caustic and subversive, the other diplomatic and virtuous. The son of an amateur dance bandleader, Paul is already set on show business stardom, however it may present itself. John decides to recruit him, despite obvious potential rivalry.

They write first songs together – mostly Buddy Holly imitations – while 'sagging off' from their respective schools at Paul's home.

'The decision was to let me be strong, or to bring him in and make the group stronger. I decided to make the group stronger.'

37

After leaving school, John spends three years at Liverpool College of Art, making no impact save with his unofficial talent for caricature. His mother, Julia, is knocked down and killed in Menlove Avenue, just a few yards from Mimi's house.

The Quarry Men are further augmented by George Harrison, 14 year-old son of a Liverpool bus-driver, whom John first patronises as 'that kid'. John's close friend is his fellow art student Stu Sutcliffe, a brilliant painter and stylistic innovator. Seeking a new name for the group, Stu writes 'Beetles' in his sketchbook. John changes it to 'Beatles' as a pun on beat music.

With Stu Sutcliffe on bass and Pete Best on drums, The Beatles - sometimes Silver Beatles - acquire a manager, Allan Williams, and engagements at night clubs in Hamburg's notorious Reeperbahn district. To last the all-night sessions, they need a vast repertoire of Rock 'n' Roll, Country-Western, ballads, even show tunes, bolstered by the ever-increasing Lennon-McCartney compositions. As at Quarry Bank, John is the ringleader - drinking, brawling, popping 'Prellys' to stay awake, once even going onstage with a lavatory seat round his neck.

They are taken up by German photographer Astrid Kirchherr, who becomes Sutcliffe's fiancée, encouraging him to comb his hair forward in 'French style' and wear round-collared Cardin suits. The prototype Beatle look is born.

Sutcliffe quits The Beatles to study art in Hamburg, and subsequently dies of a brain haemorrhage. John is devastated by his friend's death.

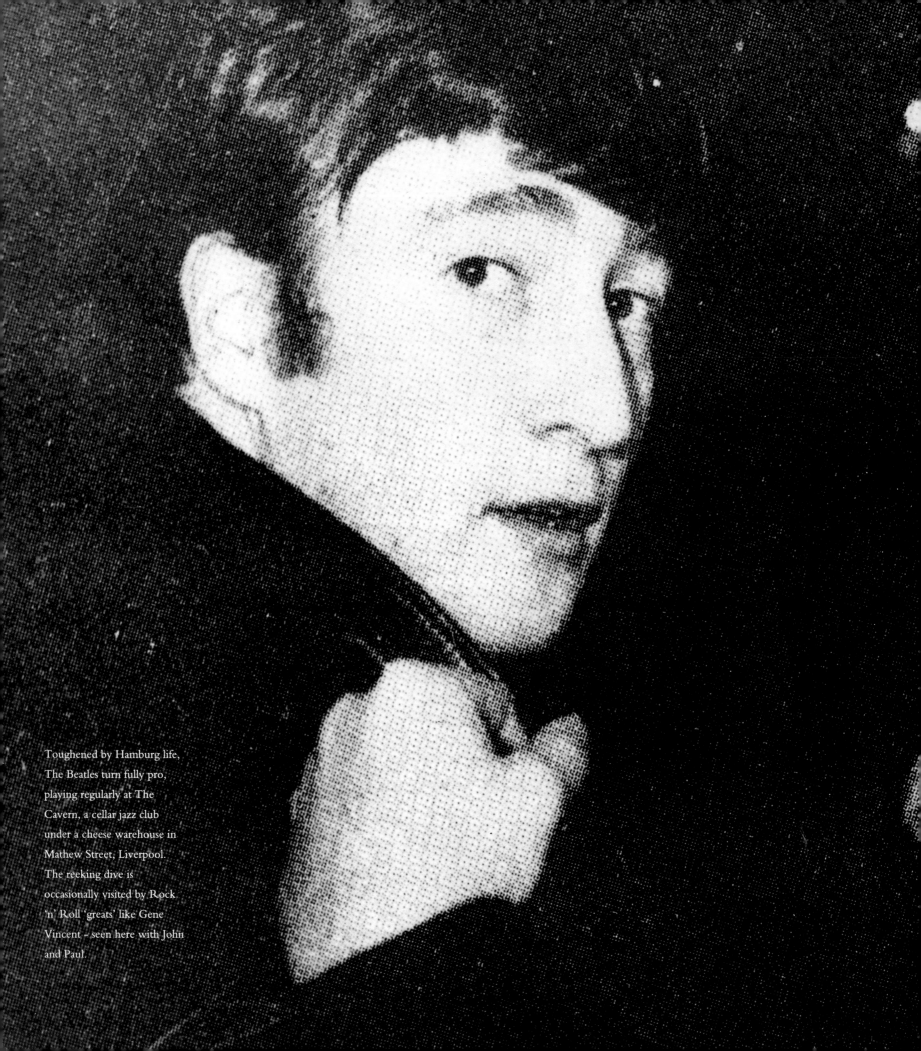

Toughened by Hamburg life,
The Beatles turn fully pro,
playing regularly at The
Cavern, a cellar jazz club
under a cheese warehouse in
Mathew Street, Liverpool.
The reeking dive is
occasionally visited by Rock
'n' Roll 'greats' like Gene
Vincent – seen here with John
and Paul.

Otumba awoke him with a cup of teeth, and they lit up towards the jumble.

"Ain't dat Elepoon Pill?" said Wipe Hudnose, "wearing his new Basuti?"

"Could be the Flying Docker on a case."

"No he's walking," said Otumba in swahily which is not arf from here as the crowbarks. All too soon they reached a cleaner in the jumble and set up cramp."

Jumble Jim, whom shall remain nameless, was slowly, but slowly asking his way through the underpants (underware he was being washed by Whide Hunter).

"Beat the bus Otumbath!" commanded Wheat Hoover.

"No, but maybie next week it will be my turn to beat the bus now standing at platforbe nine."

by Bob Dean

CLASSIFIED ADS.

Advertisements are charged at 4d. per word, minimum charge per line is 1/6d. The text should be printed or typed on plain paper and sent to "Classified Advertisements", Mersey Beat, 81a Renshaw Street, Liverpool 1. Advertisement forms are also available from the above address. The number of insertions required must be clearly stated, and a cheque enclosed to cover the cost (allow five words to the line). All advertisements must be prepaid.

ALPHA SOUND services for the best in sound reproduction. Phone: WAT 7862.

HOT LIPS, missed you Friday, RED NOSE.

It's A.1 at the A.I.

TAPE RECORDERS.—We offer 15% discount on cash purchases.—Starlac Enterprises Ltd., 17 Slater Street, Liverpool 1.

TALENT NIGHTS.—New Country and Western artists always welcome on Friday nights at the Black Cat Club.—Apply to Secretary.

RED NOSE, missed you Friday, HOT LIPS.

FOUR original Oil Paintings in superb frames. Ideal for restaurant or club. £5. Box C.3.

ACCRINGTON welcomes HOT LIPS AND RED NOSE.

THE BLUEHAWKS are coming!

BANJOIST, read or busk, wishes to join semi-pro rock, skiffle or trad. group.—Box C.4.

WANTED URGENTLY by ex-top rock group: five portable D.D.T. guns. —Box B.1.

Whistling Jock Lennon wishes to contact HOT NOSE.

Who are "Sammy and the Spoilers"?

RED SCUNTHORPE wishes to jock HOT ACCRINGTON.

You cannot "Beta" ALPHA SOUND!

GERRY AND THE PACEMAKERS APPRECIATION CLUB. Membership will be 7/6 yearly. This obtains for you a large 10" x 8" photo of fabulous GERRY AND THE PACEMAKERS plus your membership card.

In due course the club shall meet as often as possible during the week so that all Gerry's fans can call at some time or other during the week, but until the suitable premises are ...

... ... and some ... phone records (some of them Gerry's).

All Postal Orders should be made out to "Mersey Beat" and posted to 81a Renshaw Street, Liverpool 1; also all enquiries to the same address, c/o Mr. Stan Ericson.

Black leather-clad kingpins of the exploding Liverpool 'beat' scene that will also produce Gerry and the Pacemakers, Billy J. Kramer, The Searchers and Cilla Black. John finds a home for his oddball literary gift in a local music paper, *Mersey Beat*, writing a regular column as 'Beatcomber', even contributing halfpenny-a-line small ads under various aliases, 'Whistling Jock Lennon', 'Hot Lips' and 'Red Nose'.

December 1961. The Beatles agree to be managed by Brian Epstein, 27 year-old manager of his family's record and electrical shop, Nems. The streetwise boys are well aware that Epstein is a homosexual, with more or less overt designs on John. He makes them drop their Hamburg leathers in favour of smart suits reflecting his own cultivated taste. He also earns the hatred of their Cavern following by firing their 'too handsome' drummer, Pete Best. Enter Ritchie Starkey, alias Ringo Starr, formerly drummer with another Mersey group, Rory Storm and the Hurricanes.

John is uneasy about 'selling out' but goes along with the majority vote.

'The Beatles died then, as musicians. That's why we never improved as musicians. We killed ourselves, trying to make it.'

Epstein cannot at first interest any London
record company in a group from Liverpool.
Decca turns The Beatles down in favour of
Barking-based Brian Poole and the
Tremeloes.
In their Cavern prison, John is the optimist
and cheerleader.

'Where are we going, fellas?'
'To the top, Johnny!'
'Where's that, fellas?'
'The toppermost of the poppermost, Johnny!'

The obscure Parlophone label finally offers a recording contract at the Scrooge-like royalty rate of one old penny per double-sided record. Label head George Martin, a specialist in dance music and light comedy discs, becomes The Beatles' producer. The sessions, at EMI's Abbey Road studio, provide a rare glimpse of John in his detested glasses. Their debut single, Love Me Do, makes the charts - allegedly helped by Brian Epstein's purchase of 10,000 copies. Their second,

Please Please Me, goes to number one in Britain, followed by an album on which George Martin (right) captures the excitement of their Cavern stage performance.

'We ended with Twist and Shout. God knows how John managed it, because his vocal always made a sound like tearing flesh.'

A one-hit band among many, touring Britain in Pop 'package shows' with American headliners like Tommy Roe and Roy Orbison, playing live on BBC radio's Saturday Club, whose compere Brian Matthew calls them 'the most exciting group since The Shadows'.

John has flouted teen idol convention by marrying his art college girl friend, the long-suffering Cynthia Powell. This - and the rapid birth of their son, Julian - must be sedulously concealed from Beatles fans.

Between their first and second albums, a remarkable transition. The chirpy artisans, reviled by politicians and prelates, metamorphose into thoughtful, soulful studentish types whom any deb's mother would be glad to invite into the drawing room.

The repartee is like nothing ever heard in Pop before.

Reporter: 'Wasn't there a producer at Decca who turned you down?'
Paul: 'He must be kicking himself now.'
John: 'I 'ope he kicks himself to death.'

Lennon-McCartney write prolifically on the wing, amid dressing-room debris between shows. Irrespective of its progenitor, every song wears the democratic double by-line. So Paul gets credit for Norwegian Wood, and John for Yesterday.

with the beatles **stereo**

'I used to try and get George to rebel with me. I'd say to him "Look, we don't need these fuckin' suits. Let's chuck them out of the window". My little rebellion was to have my tie loose with the top button of my shirt undone. But Paul'd always come up to me and put it straight.'

MEET THE

BEATLES

STAR SPECIAL

Number Twelve

AN
INFORMAL
DATE IN
WORDS &
PERSONAL
ALBUM
PICTURES

2'6

INTRODUCED
by THEMSELVES
Written and
compiled by
TONY BARROW

The press prefer the cuddly myth, even though the reality is imperfectly concealed.

John's telegram of apology for assaulting Cavern DJ Bob Wooler at Paul's 21st birthday party (below right). Wooler had claimed John had a homosexual relationship with Brian Epstein.

'When we hit town, we hit it. There was no pissing about. There's photographs of me crawling about in Amsterdam on my knees ... coming out of whorehouses and things like that. The police escorted me to the places because they never wanted a big scandal, you see.'

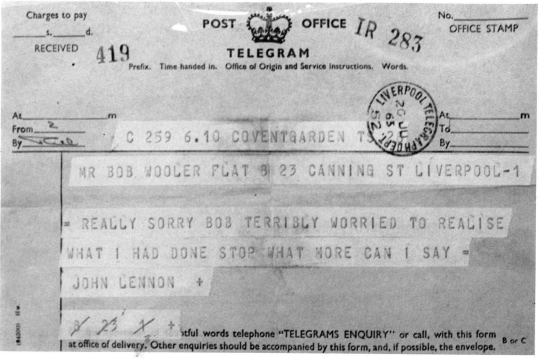

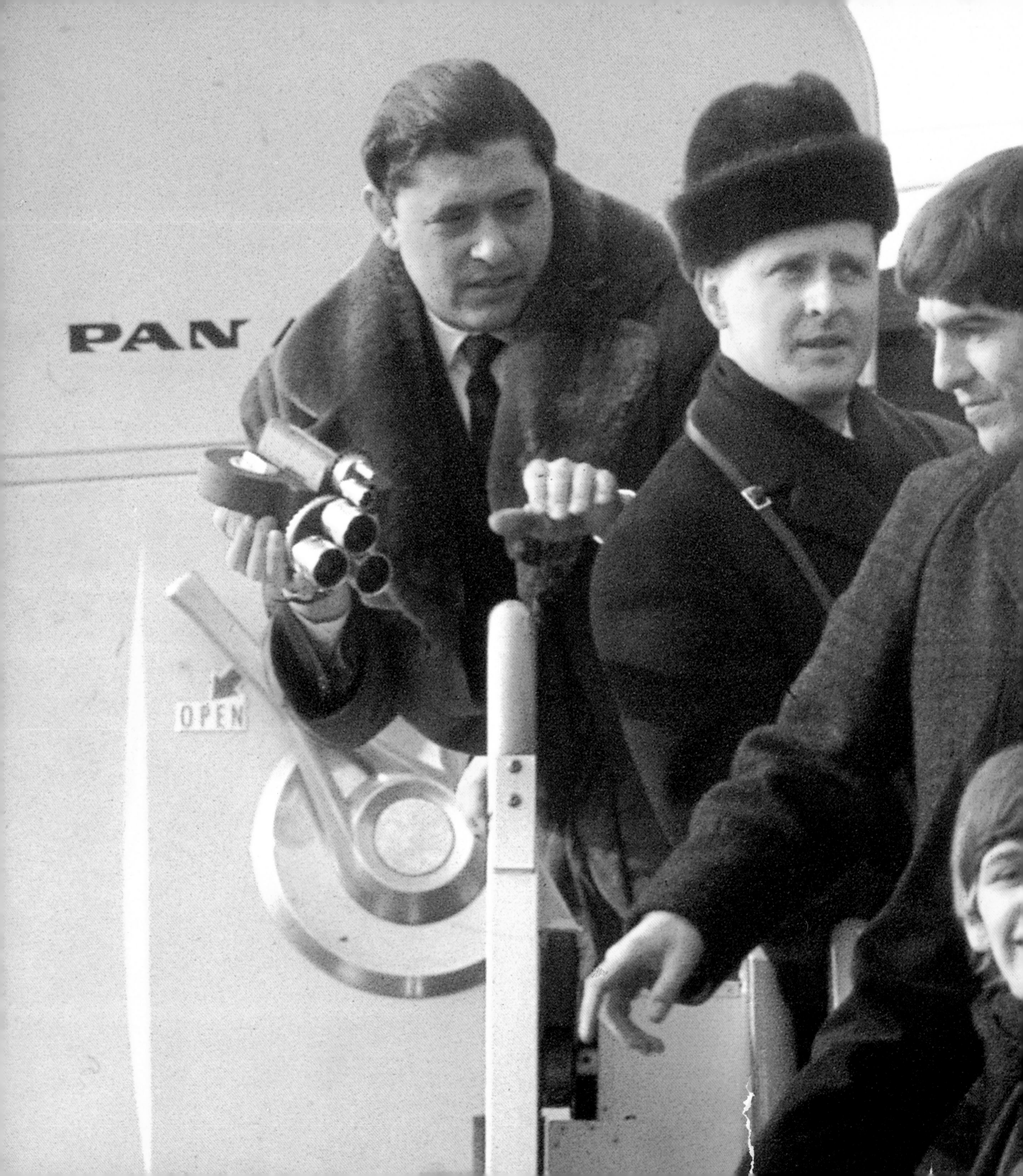
PAN
OPEN

'By the time we got to the States, we'd learned the whole game ...
We knew we could wipe you out if we could just get a grip on you.'

'I remember noticing John that first time on The Ed Sullivan Show.
He's standing there, looking around him as if to say "Is this corny or
what?" ' *Billy Joel*

American reporter:
'What is your opinion of
Americans who
go to Canada to escape
the draft?'
John: 'We're not allowed
opinions.'

The myth is made visual in their first movie, premiered before Her trendymost Royal Highness, Princess Margaret.

Reporter: 'Can we look forward to any more Beatle movies?'
John: 'Well, there'll be many more, but I don't know if you can look forward to them.'

John's first book of drawings and Goonish jottings, *John Lennon in His Own Write*, is celebrated by a Foyle's literary lunch. *The Times Literary Supplement* says that *In His Own Write* 'is worth the study of anyone who fears for the impoverishment of the English language'.

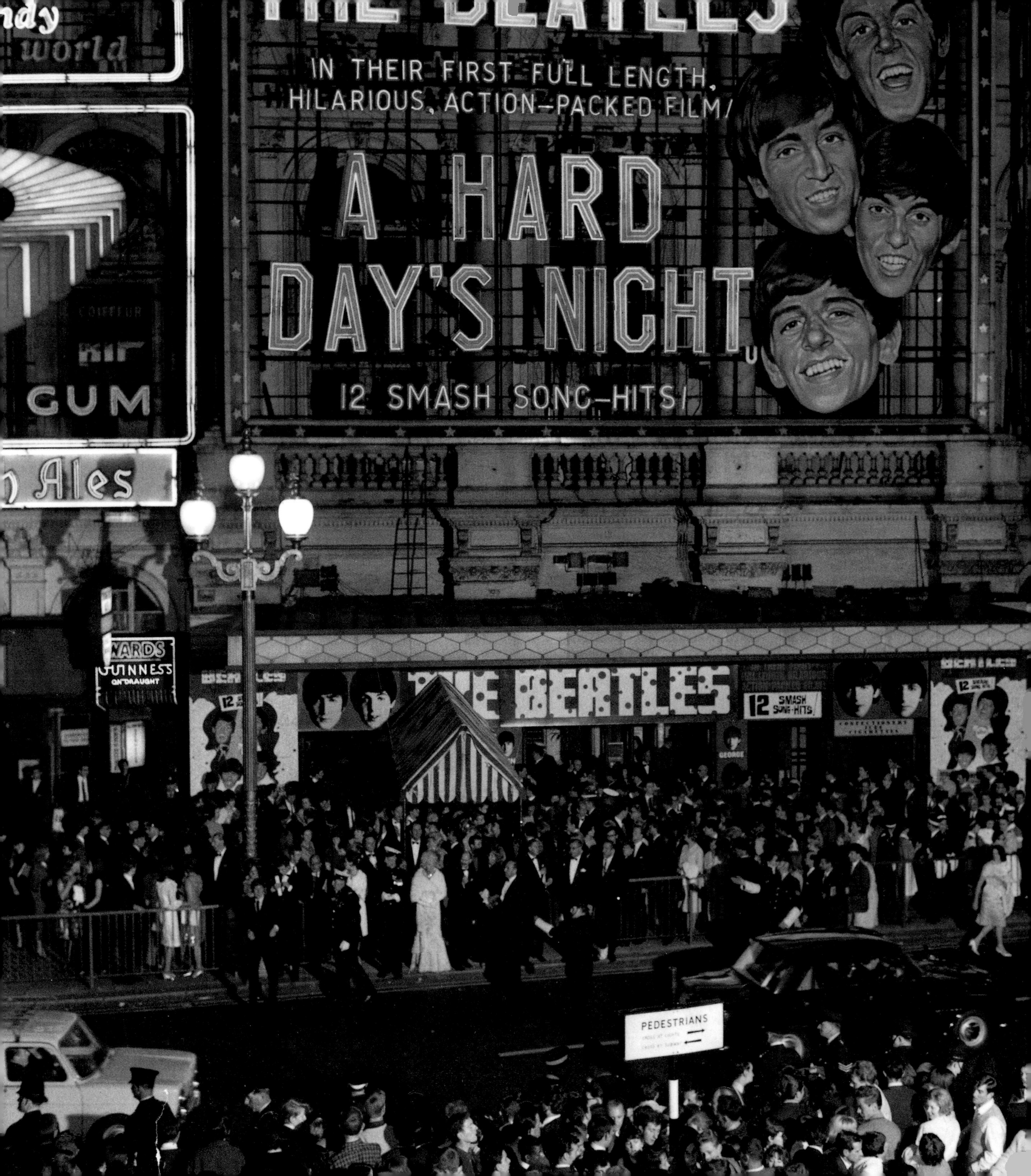
THE BEATLES
IN THEIR FIRST FULL LENGTH, HILARIOUS, ACTION-PACKED FILM!
A HARD DAY'S NIGHT
12 SMASH SONG-HITS!
GUM
Ales
GUINNESS
ON DRAUGHT
THE BEATLES
12 SMASH SONG-HITS
PEDESTRIANS

Socialist Prime Minister Harold Wilson hijacks Beatlemania as an electoral asset. On his recommendation The Queen invests The Beatles as Members of the Most Excellent Order of the British Empire. To gain courage for the ceremony, John leads a marijuana-smoking session in a Buckingham Palace washroom. 'We had to do a lot of selling out then. Taking the MBE was a sell-out for me.'
Left: 'Kenwood', the mock-Tudor mansion found for John and Cynthia by one of the Beatles' accountants.

Lennon as Lenin, droll star of *Help!*, the second Beatle movie, 1965. Envied by millions with his mansion, his riches and his pretty blonde wife – on the inside, riven with frustration and contempt for the pawn and 'Nowhere Man' he feels he has become.

'*Help!* was just bullshit. It had nothing to do with The Beatles. They just put us here and there ... we were extras in our own film.'

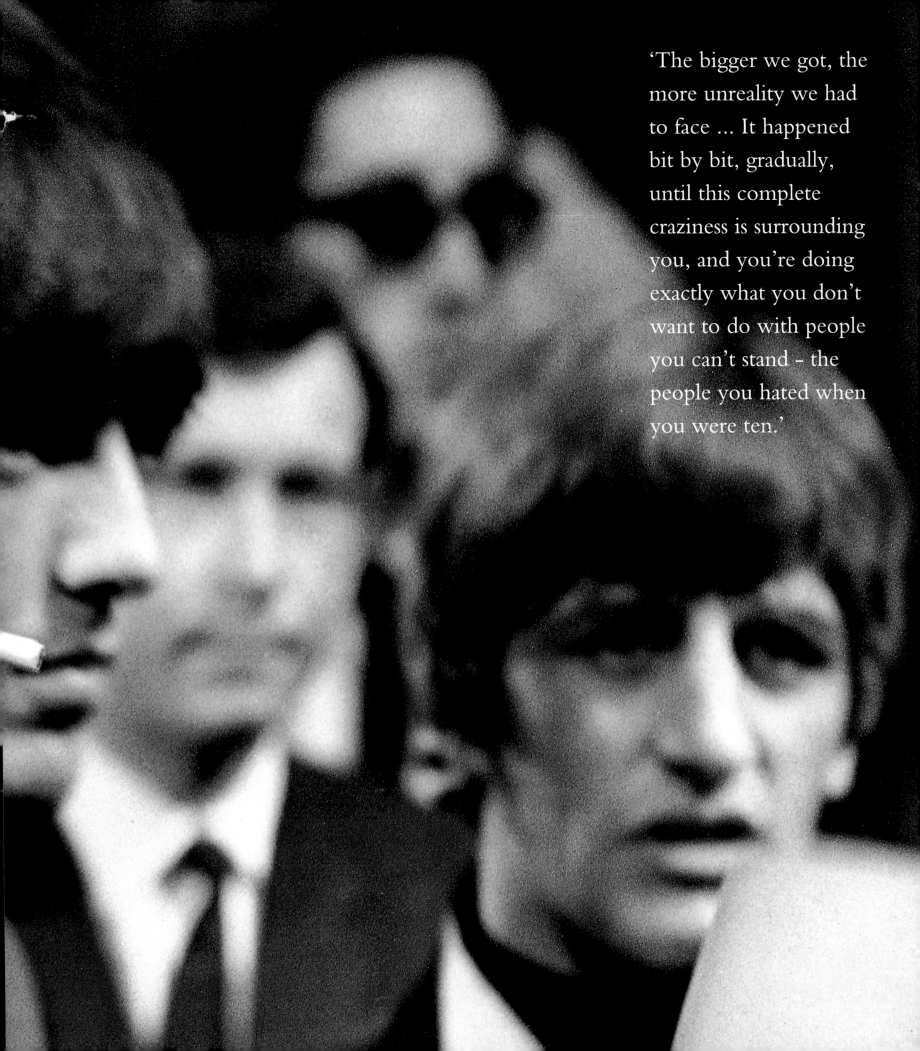

'The bigger we got, the more unreality we had to face ... It happened bit by bit, gradually, until this complete craziness is surrounding you, and you're doing exactly what you don't want to do with people you can't stand – the people you hated when you were ten.'

'Christianity will go. It will vanish and shrink ... We're more popular than Jesus now. I don't know which will go first – Rock 'n' Roll or Christianity. Jesus was all right, but his disciples were thick and ordinary. It's them twisting [The Bible] that ruins it for me.'

The backlash is worldwide. In America's Deep South, Beatles albums are ceremonially burned. On a Far East tour, The Beatles allegedly snub Imelda Marcos and are roughed up at Manila airport. After barely three years at the top, they cease to be a performing group.

In the sudden lull, John tries movie-acting – 'Private Gripweed' in *How I Won The War* – and attempts to get on terms with the son he admits he has abandoned, just as his own mother abandoned him.

He visits a London exhibition by the Japanese performance artist, Yoko Ono. She invites him to pay five shillings to climb a stepladder and hammer an imaginary nail into the ceiling. 'I'll hammer in an imaginary nail if I can give you an imaginary five shillings,' John replies.

John with George Martin during playback, 1967.
Stage ringleader turns to studio wizard, shouter to sage, pothead to acid freak. The Beatles' *Sgt. Pepper's Lonely Hearts Club Band* revolutionises the concept of the Pop LP. Though the catchy Carnaby concept is Paul's, the album lives on through two Lennon songs: Lucy In The Sky With Diamonds and, his lethargic masterpiece, A Day In The Life.

'Dylan was always saying to me "Listen to the words" and I said "I can't be bothered. I listen to the sound of it, the overall thing". Then I reversed that, and started being a words man.'

Man and car alike are psychedelic icons in 1967's horribly-misnamed Summer of Love, when The Beatles chant their simplistic anthem to a world television audience of 400 million. John leads the way in their experiments with the 'mind-expanding' drug LSD. Though denying Lucy In The Sky With Diamonds was a name-check for LSD, he afterwards admits that he 'literally ate the stuff'.

During August Bank Holiday week-end, Brian Epstein is found dead of a drug overdose at his Belgravia house. During his long disintegration, John has tried to comfort him, once sending a note to him in hospital, saying 'You know I love you ...' Brian's death leaves The Beatles vulnerable and directionless. Their *Magical Mystery Tour* film bombs in Britain and America. John is captivated by the Indian guru, Maharishi Mahesh Yogi.

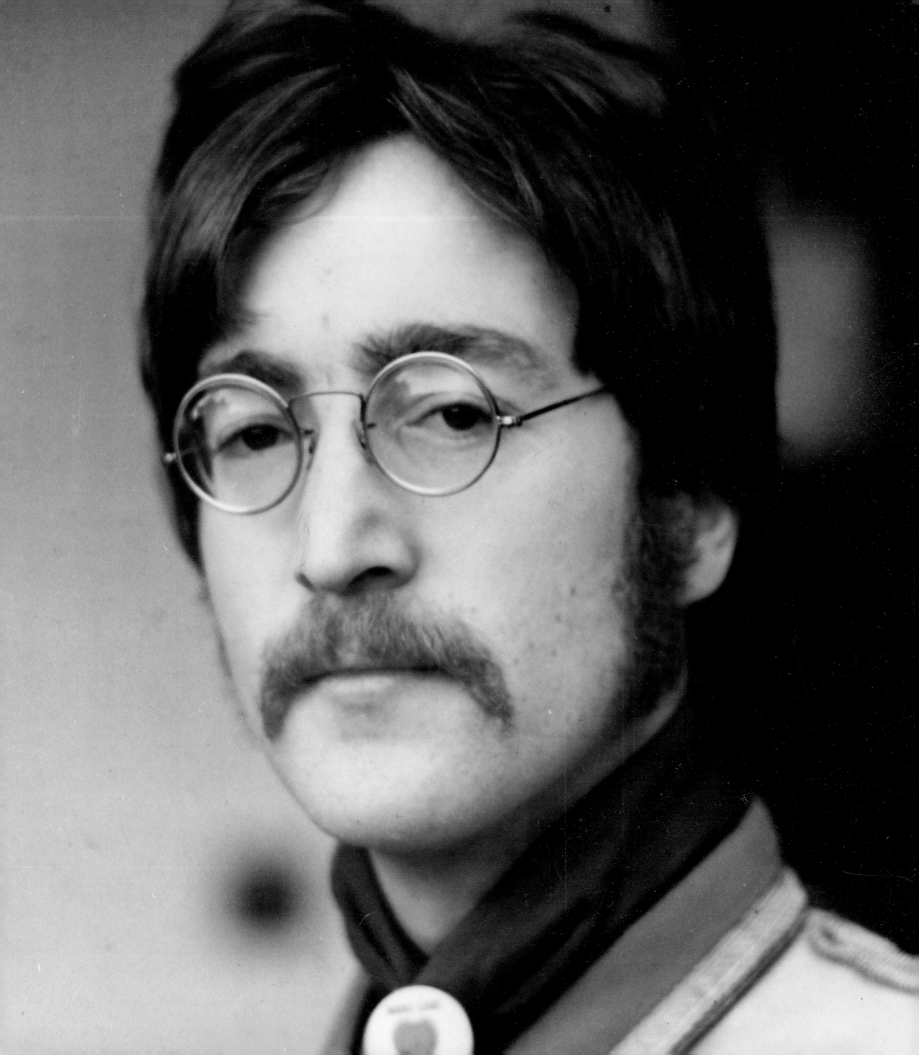

A pilgrimage to the guru's Indian ashram, however, proves less than fulfilling.

John voices the general disappointment that Maharishi has not told them the secret of life. 'Do you think if I go up in his helicopter with him, he'll slip it to me on my own?'

1968. The Beatles try to alleviate horrendous tax liabilities by sinking two million pounds into a multi-strand business named Apple, embracing music, films, electronics, publishing, clothes boutiques, even an 'Apple Foundation For The Arts' to fund creativity among their hippy brotherhood.

John is briefly reconciled to playing businessman and shop-keeper. 'The aim isn't just a stack of gold teeth in the bank ... It's more of a trick to see if we can get artistic freedom in a business structure ... if we can create things and sell them without charging five times our cost.'

After 18 months' uneasy circling, John
begins an affair with Yoko Ono while
Cynthia and Julian are on holiday in Italy.
Cynthia returns to Kenwood to find a pair
of Japanese slippers outside her bedroom
door.

'Once I started with Yoko, I had to drop
everything else. It was goodbye to the
boys in the band.'

His fans are appalled at the ruthlessness
with which Cynthia is cauterised from his
life, and instantly detest Yoko, greeting
her with cries of 'Yellow' and 'Chink'.
One doorstep 'Apple scruff' hands her a
bunch of yellow roses with the thorns
uppermost.

John holds his first art exhibition, dedicated to his new Japanese muse. While hiding out together in a flat rented by Ringo, they are raided by police, who discover 219 grains of cannabis resin. Yoko becomes pregnant by John, but suffers a miscarriage. He sleeps on the floor beside her hospital bed. Their first album together, *Two Virgins*, features them on its cover as full frontal nudes, and has to be distributed in brown paper bags.

Yoko – reluctantly accepted by the other Beatles as 'flavour of the month' – becomes involved in the business imbroglios around Apple. The venture is a financial haemorrhage which, John admits, has reduced him to his 'last fifty thousand pounds'. To manage the Beatles and sort out Apple, he appoints New York entrepreneur Allen Klein, thereby causing an irreparable rift with Paul McCartney.

1969. Thirty thousand copies of *Two Virgins* are confiscated as 'pornography' in New Jersey, USA. John and Yoko marry in Gibraltar, then hold a seven-day 'bed-in', to promote world peace, in room 902 at the Amsterdam Hilton hotel.

'We're all Christ and we're all Hitler. We're trying to make Christ's message contemporary. We want Christ to win. What would He have done if He had advertisements, records, films, TV and newspapers? Well, the miracle today is communication. So let's use it.'

'We're the new Tolpuddle Martyrs,
if you like ...'

As another temporary hideout, John buys Tittenhurst Park, near Sunningdale, Berkshire. The ever-mobile Two Virgins espouse a dozen social and political causes ... Northern Ireland, Black Muslims, vegetarianism, *Oz* magazine. They hold a second bed-in, in Montreal, Canada, and are involved in a car crash in the Scottish Highlands. 'John has the wrecked car compacted into a cube and put on show in his grounds. He returns his MBE medal to The Queen 'as a protest against Britain's involvement in the Nigeria-Biafra thing, against our support of America in Vietnam and against Cold Turkey slipping down the charts.' Lithographs by John are confiscated by police as 'obscene'. Yoko miscarries a second baby. 'Heroin? It wasn't too much fun. I never injected it or anything. We sniffed a little when we were in real pain. We took 'H' because of what The Beatles and their pals were doing to us. We were getting so much pain that we had to do something about it.'

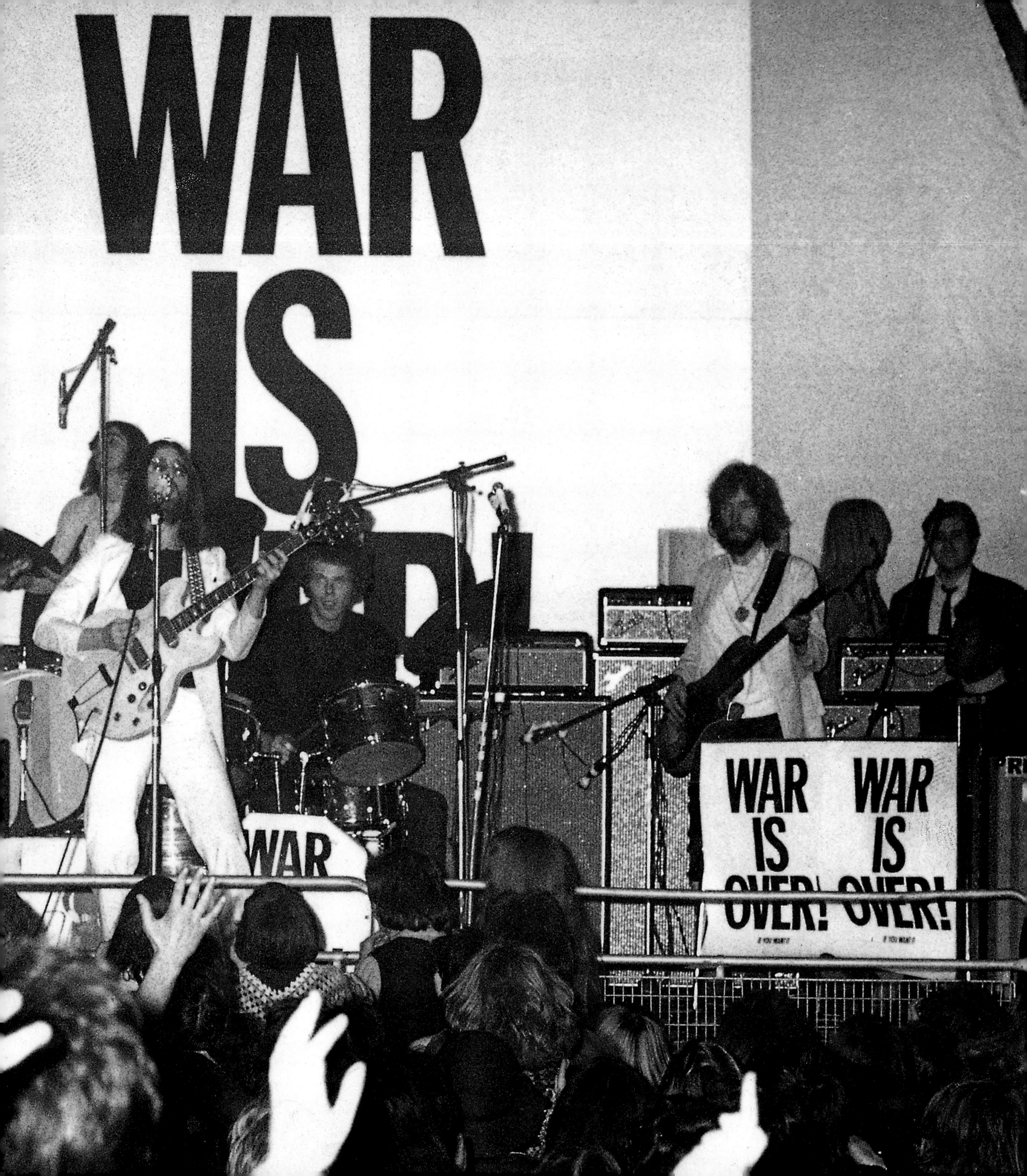
WAR
IS
WAR
WAR
IS
OVER!
WAR
IS
OVER!

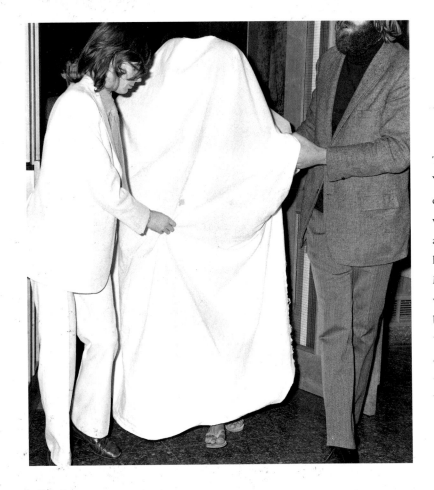

The Plastic Ono Band, John and Yoko's ad hoc supergroup, puts out old-fashioned Rock 'n' Roll with brand-new peace propaganda at the Toronto Rock festival. They have a summit meeting with Prime Minister Pierre Trudeau, afterwards describing him as 'more beautiful than we expected'.
'I don't expect the prime ministers or kings and queens of the world to suddenly change their policies because John and Yoko have said "Peace" ... It's youth we're addressing. If we can get inside their minds, we'll be satisfied.'

As John and Yoko evolve 'bagism' as a form of political protest, The Beatles record two sunset albums, the brilliant *Abbey Road* and the excruciating *Let It Be*.

'I thought it would be really good to let the shitty version out, because it would break the Beatles myth ... "This is what we are like with our trousers off. Will you please end the game now?"'

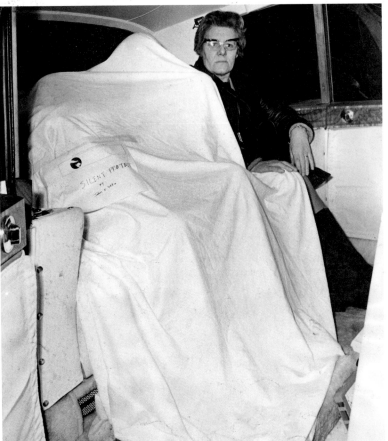

'I'd like to say thank you
on behalf of
the group and ourselves,
and I hope we passed
the audition.'

The Beatles' last concert, in
freezing cold on the Apple
roof. At least the one in ratty
fun fur is jubilant.

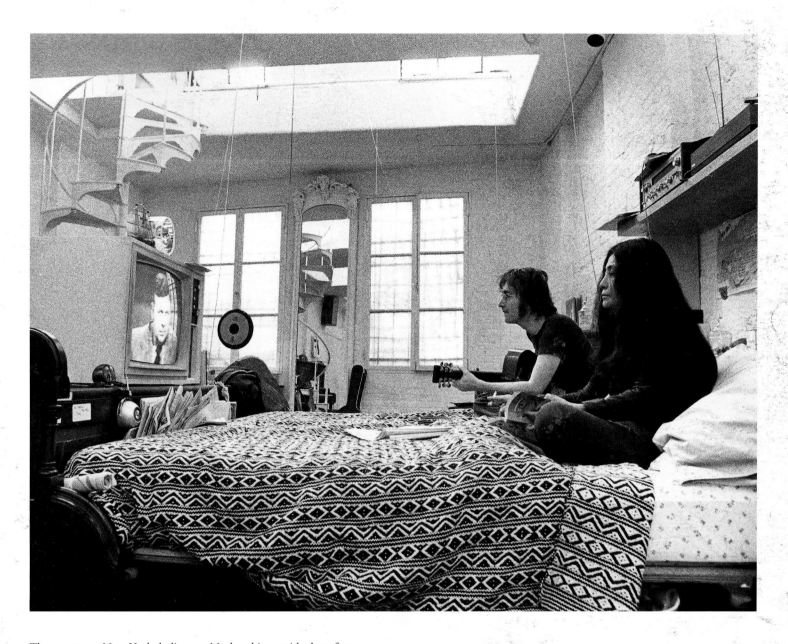

They escape to New York, holing up first in an hotel, then in a Greenwich Village loft. Walking the cobbled Downtown streets, past old warehouses with iron fire-escapes, is like returning to the Liverpool of John's childhood. The 'Primal Scream' therapy he has undergone with Arthur Janov permeates his music - especially Mother, his anguished cry from infancy for the feckless Julia.

'In England, I'm regarded as the guy who won the pools. She's regarded as the lucky Jap who married the guy who won the pools. In America we are both treated as artists.'

The feud with Paul continues in a song, How Do You Sleep?

After charity benefits with Yoko and a famous guest spot with Elton John at Madison Square Garden, John bids farewell to stage performing. Constantly revived rumours that The Beatles may re-form always receive the same withering put down.

'Why me? Why not you? Why don't you start right now and get yourself as famous as The Beatles? It's quite easy if you want to work twenty-four hours a day and keep smiling and dancing for about fifteen years. Then you can do it. Why is everybody telling me to do it? I already did it!'

John to waitress at LA
Troubadour club:
'Do you know who I am?'
Waitress: 'Yeah. An asshole
with a Kotex on his head.'

1973. John leaves Yoko at
their apartment in the Dakota
Building and goes to Los
Angeles for the drunken and
confused eight months he
will subsequently call his 'lost
weekend'. On a not untypical
night, he is thrown out of the
Troubadour for heckling
comedian Tommy Smothers.

'He was a miserable drunk,' his friend
Elliott Mintz recalls. 'One brandy Alexander
and he was absolutely delightful. Two was
okay. Three, and he started snarling.'

Reunion with Yoko and the birth of their son, Sean Taro Ono Lennon. John wins his long battle against deportation by the US Immigration authorities, being awarded a Green Card with the option of applying for full citizenship in 1981.

While Yoko administers their finances, John gives up music to become a 'househusband' and raise Sean.

'He didn't come out of my belly but, by God, I made his bones, because I've attended to every meal, and to how he sleeps, and to the fact that he swims like a fish. That's because I took him to the 'Y'. I took him to the ocean. He's my biggest pride.'

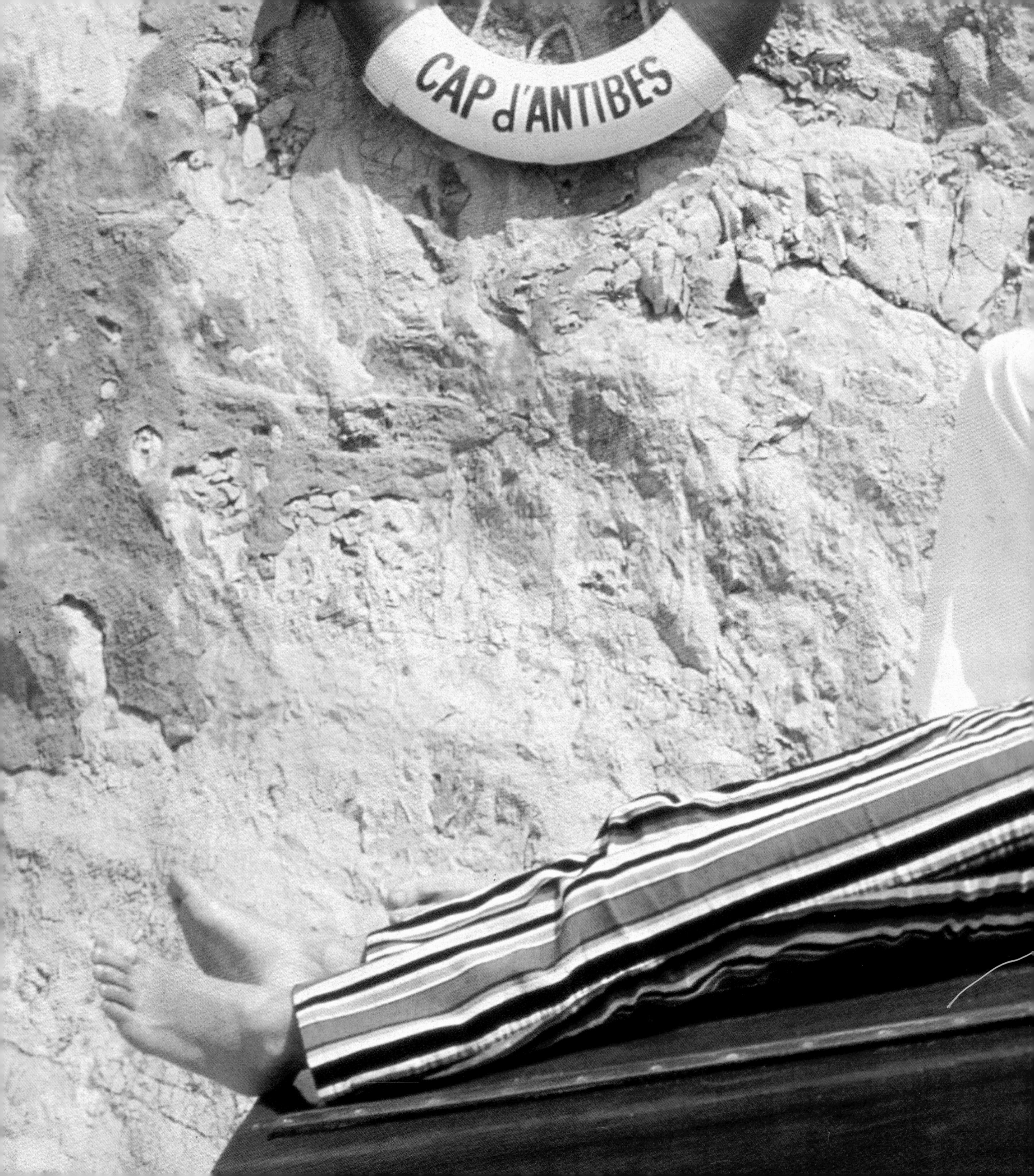
CAP d'ANTIBES

'A few days before it happened,

I remember looking at John. And he looked so good,

so beautiful. I remember thinking

"I wonder if things can go on being as good as this?" '

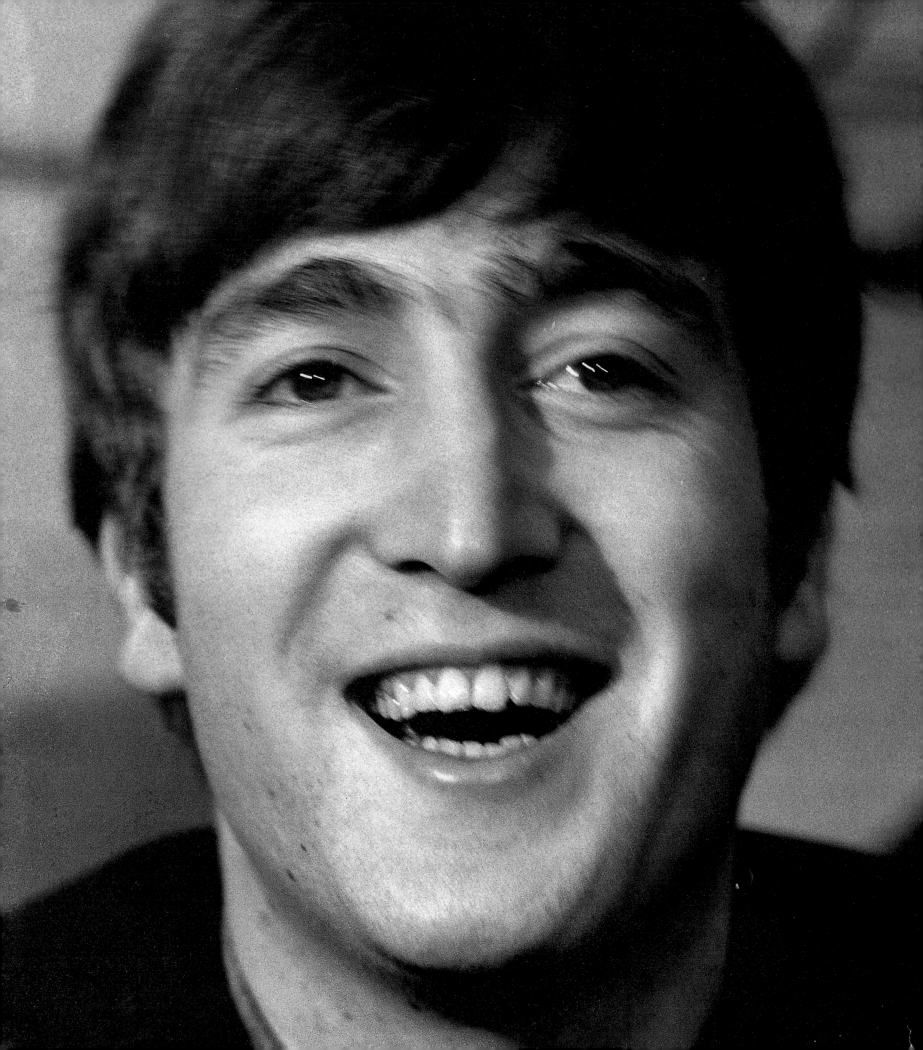

Pictorial Press
Front Cover, 2, 4-5, 22, 36-37, 38, 40-41, 46,53, 58, 59, 60, 61 top, 68, 69, 70, 72 top, 74-75,
82 bottom, 84-85, 88-89, 90 bottom, 108-109 Bob Gruen

Rex Features
28, 32, 42-43, 45, 48-49, 61, 65, 66-67, 78, 79, 87, 92-93, 94, 104, 105, 106 Kishin Shinoyama,
107, 111 Kishin Shinoyama, 110, 112-113

Retna
62-63 Bob Freeman

Magnum,
David Hurn 7, 14, 15, 16, 23, 116, 119, Back Cover
D. McCullin 17, 18, 99
Philip Jones Griffiths 24, 117
Anita Hoffman 21, 102
Alex Webb 120

Popperfoto
8-9, 26, 27, 31, 34, 35, 39, 41, 47, 50, 52, 56-57, 64, 71, 90, 98

Camera Press
12, 20, 30, 33, 54-55, 76, 77, 80, 86, 88, 91, 95, 101 Ethan A. Russell, 103, 118 Terence Spencer

London Features International
10, 50, 82, 96-97
David Bailey 115
Laurie 73